DON'T WAIT JUST CREATE

SHUBHAM MEENA

AF487369

Copyright © SHUBHAM MEENA
All Rights Reserved.

This book has been self-published with all reasonable efforts taken to make the material error-free by the author. No part of this book shall be used, reproduced in any manner whatsoever without written permission from the author, except in the case of brief quotations embodied in critical articles and reviews.

The Author of this book is solely responsible and liable for its content including but not limited to the views, representations, descriptions, statements, information, opinions and references ["Content"]. The Content of this book shall not constitute or be construed or deemed to reflect the opinion or expression of the Publisher or Editor. Neither the Publisher nor Editor endorse or approve the Content of this book or guarantee the reliability, accuracy or completeness of the Content published herein and do not make any representations or warranties of any kind, express or implied, including but not limited to the implied warranties of merchantability, fitness for a particular purpose. The Publisher and Editor shall not be liable whatsoever for any errors, omissions, whether such errors or omissions result from negligence, accident, or any other cause or claims for loss or damages of any kind, including without limitation, indirect or consequential loss or damage arising out of use, inability to use, or about the reliability, accuracy or sufficiency of the information contained in this book.

Made with ♥ on the Notion Press Platform
www.notionpress.com

This book is dedicated to all those who have ever found themselves standing at the crossroads of uncertainty, doubting their potential, and waiting for the right moment to act. To the dreamers who wonder if their goals are ever within reach, to those who have felt the weight of procrastination, and to the ones who have watched time slip away, wishing they had started sooner.

But more than anything, this is dedicated to you—the ones who are ready to rise above the fear of failure, the ones who are prepared to take that first step no matter how small it may seem. This is for those who believe that their future is shaped by the actions they take today, and who understand that the power to change lies within them.

May this book inspire you to stop waiting for the perfect time and start creating the life you deserve, today. The journey may not always be easy, but with each step, you are one step closer to becoming the person you are meant to be.

So, to you—the dreamers, the warriors, the doers—this book is for you. Never stop striving for more, and remember: your story is only beginning.

Contents

FOREWORD

This book is about one simple truth- **action creates change**. Dreams remain dreams unless we take the first step toward them. Fear, doubt, and hesitation hold us back, but only action moves us forward.

I wrote this book to inspire you take that step. No matter how small, every action bring you closer to your goal. **Don't just think-act. Don't just dream-do.**

Letthis book be your reminder that the only way to progress is to move.

Shubham Meena

Preface

Sometimes, a single moment changes everything. For me, that moment came unexpectedly, hidden within the lyrics of a song— "Dil me jo aye, aaj ho jaye." (Whatever comes to your heart, let it happen today.)

At first, it felt like just another line from a song, something we hear and forget. But this time, it stayed with me. I kept thinking—what if we truly lived by these words? What if we stopped overthinking, stopped waiting for the 'right time,' and just acted on what we truly wanted? How different would life be if we dared to take risks instead of holding back?

This single thought set off a chain reaction in my mind. I began questioning the fears, doubts, and excuses that stop us from making decisions. I started noticing how we often hesitate, overanalyze, and let opportunities slip away. That's when I realized—I had to write this book.

This isn't just a story. It's a conversation, a journey through choices, risks, and the power of taking action. Through these pages, I want to take you along with me—to explore, to question, and most importantly, to act.

So, are you ready? Because this time, hesitation is not an option.

Acknowledgements

This book is the result of my own thoughts , efforts, and dedication. No one assisted me in this journey, and every word written here is solely my own. I thank myself for the perseverance and determination that led to the completion of this book.

I

WHY NOT TODAY

Be honest—how many times have you told yourself, "I'll start tomorrow"?

Maybe you wanted to start working out, learn a new skill, or finally take that big step in life. But instead, you whispered, "Not today. Maybe later."

And then?

That "tomorrow" never comes.

The Power of Procrastination

Procrastination, man. We all know about it, right? Most of the time, we think procrastination is just that bad habit that keeps us from getting things done. But here's the twist—what if procrastination actually has some power? Sounds weird, right? But seriously, we might be looking at it all wrong.

Let's break it down:

Imagine you have this big task—something important. And you're like, "Yeah, I'll just take a little more time and get to it later." You think you're wasting time, but actually, procrastination has its own logic. We all do it—our mind convinces us that "Hey, this can wait. It's not that important right now." But the truth is, we just wanna stay in our comfort zone. Hmm, right?

Why Do We Procrastinate?

Fear of failure – Oh, we all know this one. We don't want to start because we're scared that we might fail. "What if I mess it up?" So, we avoid it altogether.

Perfectionism – Ah, the classic! We want everything to be perfect, so we end up planning forever and never really start. Oh shit! This gets us nowhere.

Lack of motivation – Sometimes the task seems boring, or we don't see the reward. So we convince ourselves, "I'll do it tomorrow." Hahaha, we've all been there, right?

The Hidden Power of Procrastination

Now, here's the thing—we usually think of procrastination as a bad thing. But guess what? It has some hidden superpowers that we might not even be aware of. Let's look at this:

1. Creativity Boosts

When you put something off, your brain is still working on it. You might not be aware of it, but taking a break from the task can sometimes lead to new ideas. You know, even great minds like Leonardo da Vinci were procrastinators! He used to think, "Let me wait a bit, then I'll come up with a better idea."

2. Better Decision Making

Hmm, interesting. When you procrastinate, you're actually giving yourself more time to think about things. That means you're not rushing into decisions. When we rush, we tend to make mistakes.

3. Increased Efficiency Under Pressure

Okay, everyone knows this—when the deadline is looming, we perform our best. There's something about pressure that makes us get into this zone where we focus and get things done. Procrastination sometimes leads to that moment when you're like, "I gotta get this done NOW," and boom, you crush it.

4. Prioritization

Here's another cool thing: when you procrastinate, you end up prioritizing your tasks subconsciously. If something keeps getting pushed to the back burner, it probably wasn't as important as you thought. Procrastination can force you to focus on what really matters.

5. Mental Recovery

Sometimes, you need to step back. Procrastination can actually help your mental recovery. We're constantly on the go, and by postponing something, we're giving ourselves a chance to relax and recharge. When we're fresh, we're more productive.

How to Use Procrastination to Your Advantage?

Okay, so how do we make procrastination work for us? Because if we're being real, procrastination can be a pretty powerful tool if you use it the right way. Let's dive in.

1. Structured Procrastination

This is a trick where you delay important tasks, but you end up doing other productive things. For example, if you're putting off a big project, you might end up checking your emails, organizing your desk, or doing a smaller task that's still important. So, procrastination still leads to productivity.

2. The 5-Minute Rule

Here's a simple rule: Commit to just 5 minutes of work. You'll be surprised how quickly you get into the zone. Once you start, you'll likely continue working much longer than planned.

3. Reflect During the Delay

When you procrastinate, it's a good time to reflect on the task. You can rethink your strategies, goals, and plan. It's like a 'thinking' time that can be productive too. So, procrastination can be your opportunity to reassess.

4. Pairing with Enjoyable Tasks

This is something I do all the time! When you have something boring to do, pair it with something you enjoy. Listen to your favorite music or have a snack while you work. It makes procrastination more fun and less stressful.

When Procrastination Becomes Dangerous

Now, let's be real. Procrastination is great when it's under control. But when it starts to mess with your life—when you miss deadlines, the quality of your work drops, and stress piles up—that's when it's a problem.

Conclusion: Embrace It, But Use It Wisely

Here's the deal—don't completely eliminate procrastination. It has its benefits, but you need to manage it. If you learn how to control it, procrastination can actually work in your favor. Just make sure you're not wasting time and using it productively.

So, the next time you find yourself procrastinating, remember to ask yourself, "Am I wasting time, or am I giving my brain the space to come up with better ideas?" Use procrastination wisely, man!

Action vs Excuse

We all have that moment, right? We set a goal, get excited about it, and then... we put it off. Why? Because we have excuses. Excuses are like that comfort blanket we wrap ourselves in whenever things get tough or uncomfortable. And let's be honest—we all have them. You know, "I'll start tomorrow," or "I'm too tired," or "It's not the right time yet." It's easy to get caught up in the habit of making excuses, but what if I told you that action is what actually gets results, not excuses?

Let's get real about excuses:

Excuses are like little stories we tell ourselves to justify why we can't do something. They're a cop-out. Think about it: when you make an excuse, you're basically saying, "I'm not going to take responsibility for this, so I'll blame something else." Damn, right? We've all been there. But here's the thing—excuses keep you stuck. They keep you in the same place, never moving forward.

You want to lose weight? "I don't have time to work out."

You want to write a book? "I'm too busy with other things."

You want to start your own business? "The economy's bad right now."

Sounds familiar? Yeah, because we all have our reasons for not doing things. We try to convince ourselves that it's not our fault. But if we keep using excuses, we'll never make progress.

Why do we make excuses?

Now, you might be thinking, "But Shubham, why do I make excuses in the first place?" Well, let's break it down.

1. Fear of failure

Fear is the biggest reason why we make excuses. It's easy to say, "I'll do it tomorrow" instead of facing the possibility of failure today. We're afraid that if we try and fail, we'll look stupid or feel bad about ourselves. So, what do we do?

We avoid it.

Example: Ever put off starting something because you were scared it wouldn't turn out the way you imagined? That's fear in action. We avoid the risk of failure by making excuses, but the real failure comes from not trying.

2. Perfectionism

If you've ever found yourself saying, "I'll do it when everything is perfect," then you're a perfectionist (and don't worry, we all have a little perfectionist in us). Perfectionism is one of the biggest excuses for not taking action. We want everything to be just right before we start, but the problem is that nothing is ever perfect.

Example: You want to start a YouTube channel, but you're waiting for the perfect camera, the perfect lighting, the perfect editing skills. Newsflash: perfection doesn't exist. The best way to get better is to start, fail, and learn.

3. Lack of time

"I don't have time to do that." This is probably the most common excuse. Let's be honest, we all make it. But here's the catch—time is the one thing we all have the same amount of. It's not about not having time; it's about how we manage it. If something is truly important to you, you'll make time for it.

Example: You say you don't have time to exercise, but somehow, you find time to scroll through Instagram for hours. Prioritize your time. Excuses like "I don't have time" just show that it's not a priority for you.

4. Comfort zone

It's super easy to stay in your comfort zone. The unknown is scary. And that's why we make excuses. It's easier to stay in the same place than to take action and risk stepping into the unknown. The idea of growth, progress, and change can be overwhelming. But growth doesn't happen in your comfort zone.

Example: You want to apply for a new job, but the idea of leaving your current one makes you uncomfortable. So, you make excuses like "I'm not qualified enough" or "I'll never get that job." But guess what? You'll never know unless you take action.

Action: The Real Game Changer

Now, let's talk about action. Action is what separates those who achieve their goals from those who don't. It's easy to say, "I want this" or "I'll do that," but without action, it's just wishful thinking. Taking action is what gets things done. It's the fuel that moves the engine forward.

When you take action, you stop talking about what you want to do and actually do it. It's simple—action leads to results. You can talk about your dreams all day, but unless you take steps towards them, they'll remain just that: dreams.

Example: Let's say you want to start a blog. You can sit around all day thinking about it, but unless you actually write that first post, you're never going to get anywhere. Action is the first step toward success.

How to Switch from Excuses to Action?

Okay, so here's the million-dollar question: "How do I stop making excuses and start taking action?" Here are a few tips to help you switch gears:

1. Break it down

Big tasks can seem intimidating, and that's why we make excuses. But if you break down your goals into smaller, manageable steps, they become less overwhelming. Instead of saying, "I have to write a book," say, "Today, I'll write 500 words." This makes it easier to take action without getting stuck in your head.

2. Start small

Taking action doesn't mean you have to do everything at once. Start with small steps. **It's like working out—**you don't need to run a marathon on day one, but if you start with a short jog, you'll gradually build momentum.

3. Set deadlines

Deadlines are crucial. They give you something concrete to work towards. Deadlines create urgency, and urgency forces you to take action. If you don't set deadlines for yourself, you'll keep making excuses.

Example: Instead of saying, "I'll finish this project sometime this week," say, "I'll finish this project by Friday."

4. Get uncomfortable

If you want to make progress, you have to get out of your comfort zone. It's not going to be easy. It's going to be uncomfortable at times. But the more you embrace discomfort, the more you'll grow.

Example: Starting a new workout routine can be tough, but the discomfort you feel in the beginning is what will lead to results in the long run.

5. Eliminate distractions

We all have distractions that keep us from taking action—social media, Netflix, YouTube, you name it. If you really want to take action, you need to cut the distractions out. Set your phone aside, turn off notifications, and give your task your full attention.

6. Change your mindset

One of the biggest reasons we make excuses is because of our mindset. We often tell ourselves, "I can't do this," or "It's too hard." Shift your mindset to one that focuses on progress, not perfection. Don't say, "I'll never be able to do this," instead say, "I'll figure it out as I go."

Conclusion: Action is the Key

At the end of the day, it's all about taking action. Excuses might feel comfortable in the moment, but they hold you back from reaching your true potential. If you want to make progress in your life, you need to stop making excuses and start taking action. It's as simple as that. Every successful person out there has faced challenges, obstacles, and fears—but they didn't let those excuses stop them. They took action. So, what are you waiting for? Stop making excuses, and start doing.

Small Step, Big Impact

Hey, so let's talk about something that many people often overlook – the power of small steps. You might think that to make a big impact, you need to take huge, bold actions. But the reality is quite different. It's the little things you do every single day that add up to create something extraordinary.

Think about it – every successful person you know didn't get there overnight. They didn't wake up and suddenly have everything figured out. Instead, they took small steps consistently, and those tiny actions started to compound into massive results.

The Compound Effect

Let me explain this with a simple analogy. Imagine you're climbing a mountain. It seems impossible at first, right? But instead of looking at the entire mountain, you focus on the next step in front of you. And after a while, you start gaining altitude without even realizing how far you've come.

This is called the Compound Effect. It's the principle where small, consistent actions—over time—lead to big results. Whether it's exercising for 15 minutes a day, saving a small amount of money each month, or reading a few pages of a book every day. Those small actions add up, and over time, they lead to something huge.

You might be thinking, "But these steps are so small! Will they really make a difference?" Here's the truth – small actions are powerful because they create momentum. Once you start moving, it's much easier to keep going. A tiny step today becomes a massive leap tomorrow.

Why Small Steps Matter More Than Big Leaps

1. Consistency Over Intensity You've probably heard people say, "Go big or go home!" or, "If you want to achieve something, aim for big goals!" While big goals are great, they often overwhelm us. The problem with thinking that you need a huge change to make an impact is that it can paralyze you. When you think you need to make a massive leap, it's easy to get discouraged if you don't achieve it right away.

Small steps, on the other hand, are easy to take. They don't require you to make huge sacrifices, and they don't overwhelm you. The key is to be consistent. It's not about doing something big once; it's about doing something small consistently. Over time, those small steps will lead to bigger and better outcomes.

Let's take an example: If you decided to work out for just 15 minutes every day, it might not seem like much at first. But if you keep doing this every single day, a month from now, you'll have spent over 7 hours working out. That's a lot more than someone who might have gone all in for one intense workout but then quit after a week because it was too much.

2. The Snowball Effect Small steps create momentum, and momentum is a game-changer. Imagine rolling a snowball down a hill. It starts small, but as it picks up speed,

it grows bigger and bigger. The more momentum you build, the easier it becomes to keep going.

This is how small steps work in life. Once you start doing something, the habit becomes stronger, and your confidence grows. You begin to see results, which motivates you to keep going, and before you know it, you've achieved more than you ever thought possible.

Example: Let's say you want to write a book. If you try to write 10,000 words in one day, you might burn out quickly. But if you write just 300 words every day, you'll have written over 9,000 words in a month. Small steps like this make it easier to build momentum without feeling overwhelmed.

3. Building Habits That Stick Another reason small steps have such a big impact is because they help you build lasting habits. When you try to make drastic changes all at once, it's easy to fall back into old patterns. But if you start small, you're more likely to stick with it.

Why? Because small steps are less intimidating. They don't feel like a huge life overhaul. And as you continue to take those small actions, they start to become part of your routine. You don't have to think about them anymore. Over time, these habits become automatic, and that's where the real change happens.

4. No Overwhelm, Just Progress One of the biggest reasons people don't take action is because they feel overwhelmed. When they look at a huge goal, it seems impossible to achieve. But breaking that big goal down into small, manageable tasks makes it feel doable.

Imagine wanting to lose weight. If you think, "I have to lose 20 pounds," it sounds like an impossible task. But if you focus on taking small steps—like eating healthier today or walking for 20 minutes—you'll feel accomplished every day, and that sense of progress builds over time. Suddenly, losing 20 pounds doesn't feel so daunting anymore.

5. The Power of Incremental Progress Here's the thing – every small step you take is an investment in your future. Every time you read a chapter of a book, every time you take a walk or choose healthy food, you're making progress. Over time, those little actions add up. You might not see the results immediately, but trust me, they're coming. The key is to stay consistent and trust the process.

How to Use Small Steps for Big Impact in Your Life:
Now that you understand the power of small steps, how can you apply this in your life? Here are a few tips:

1. Start Small, But Start The key is to start. Don't wait for the perfect moment or the perfect plan. Just take the first step. Even if it's tiny, just get started. Over time, that's what will build momentum.

2. Set Tiny, Achievable Goals Break your big goals down into smaller, achievable tasks. For example, if you want to start exercising, don't commit to an hour at the gym right away. Start with 10 minutes. The point is to make it so easy that you can't say no to it.

3. Track Your Progress Keep track of your small wins. Whether it's a journal, a habit tracker, or an app, seeing your progress will encourage you to keep going. And trust me, it feels amazing when you look back at how far you've come.

4. Be Patient Remember, change doesn't happen overnight. Give yourself time to see the results of your small steps. And don't get discouraged if you don't see immediate results. Stay focused on the process, not the outcome.

5. Celebrate the Small Wins Celebrate each small step you take. It could be as simple as acknowledging that you

made progress or treating yourself to something small when you reach a goal. This reinforces the habit and keeps you motivated.

Conclusion

To wrap it up, small steps really do lead to big impacts. The key is to stay consistent and keep moving forward, no matter how small the action seems. Success doesn't come from one giant leap—it's built on the foundation of tiny, everyday actions that add up over time.

So, remember: don't wait for the "big moment." Start small, take consistent action, and before you know it, you'll look back and realize just how far you've come. Keep going, and keep making those small steps towards your goals—because, trust me, they will have a huge impact in the long run!

Fear of Imperfections

Alright, let's talk about something that we all deal with but rarely admit: fear of imperfections. You know, that nagging voice inside your head that tells you you're not good enough, that you're not perfect, or that you shouldn't even try because things won't turn out as they should. Sound familiar? Yeah, most of us have been there.

But here's the thing—imperfections are not your enemy. In fact, they might just be the key to your growth, creativity, and success. Still, it's hard to embrace them, right? It's tough to ignore the pressure we feel from society, social media, or even ourselves to be flawless in every way.

Let's get into it: why do we fear imperfections, and why should we stop?

The Roots of Fear of Imperfections

Fear of imperfection is rooted in a deep-seated need for validation and acceptance. We live in a world where perfection is often celebrated. Whether it's the flawless photos on Instagram, the curated lives of celebrities, or the idea that "success" means being without flaws, we're constantly bombarded with unrealistic standards.

When we compare ourselves to these images of perfection, we start feeling like we don't measure up. It's easy to believe that if we aren't perfect, we won't be accepted, loved, or successful. So, we shy away from trying new things, from taking risks, and from showing up as our real selves.

Think about it—when was the last time you hesitated to share something because you were afraid of being judged? Maybe it was a piece of writing, a drawing, a presentation, or just expressing your opinion. The fear of being imperfect keeps you stuck, afraid to move forward.

Perfection vs. Excellence

First, let's clear something up. There's a difference between perfection and excellence. Perfection is unattainable and unrealistic, while excellence is about doing your best, giving your all, and learning from your mistakes.

Perfection, in its truest form, is like chasing a mirage. You think you're close, but every time you take a step toward it, it gets farther away. On the other hand, excellence is about growth and improvement. It's about striving to get better, learning, failing, and trying again. Excellence can be achieved over time, while perfection is just a mental trap.

For example, when you see an athlete training, they're not aiming for perfection. They're aiming for excellence. Sure, they might miss the target sometimes or fall short of their goals, but each time they get back up and push forward, they improve. That's what it's all about.

The Damaging Effects of Perfectionism

Let's be honest, this whole perfectionist mentality isn't doing you any favors. It's causing more harm than good. Here's why:

1. Procrastination: Ever felt like you just couldn't start a task because it had to be perfect? So, you wait... and wait... and wait, until it's too late to even try? Yup, that's the perfectionism trap. You get so caught up in wanting things to be perfect that you end up doing nothing at all. This paralyzing fear stops you from making progress and getting things done.

2. Constant Self-Doubt: When you're constantly trying to meet impossible standards, you start doubting yourself. Every mistake, every imperfection, becomes a sign that you're not good enough. This self-criticism can drain your energy, mess with your confidence, and prevent you from seeing how far you've actually come.

3. Burnout: Perfectionism often leads to overworking. You spend so much time trying to get things just right that you burn out. You exhaust yourself mentally and physically, and when things still don't turn out as perfectly as you imagined, it leaves you feeling empty and defeated.

4. Missed Opportunities: The fear of imperfection can cause you to miss out on great opportunities. Whether it's because you're afraid to speak up, take a chance, or put yourself out there, this fear holds you back from experiencing new things and growing. You might end up staying stuck in your comfort zone because you're too afraid to fail.

5. Damaged Relationships: When you're constantly striving for perfection, it can affect your relationships too. You might expect too much from others or even project your fear of imperfection onto them. In turn, this can lead to frustration, misunderstandings, and conflicts.

How to Overcome the Fear of Imperfection

Okay, so now that we've identified the problem, let's talk about how to deal with it. Overcoming the fear of imperfection isn't about stopping mistakes or becoming flawless. It's about learning to embrace your imperfections and seeing them as part of your journey.

Here are some steps to help you along the way:

1. Accept That Perfection is a Lie: The first step is to acknowledge that perfection doesn't exist. No one is perfect, and neither are you. The sooner you stop chasing it, the sooner you'll feel free to pursue your dreams without worrying about every little detail.

Remember: It's okay to fail, and it's okay to make mistakes. In fact, mistakes are often the best teachers.

2. Shift Your Focus to Progress: Instead of focusing on being perfect, focus on making progress. Take small steps toward improvement each day, and celebrate the progress you make. By doing this, you'll shift your attention away from perfection and onto the journey itself.

3. Embrace Vulnerability: One of the most powerful things you can do is allow yourself to be vulnerable. Stop hiding behind a perfect image or pretending everything's fine. Be real. Be honest. When you allow yourself to be imperfect, you create space for growth. You also give others permission to do the same, which can lead to deeper connections and a greater sense of self-worth.

4. Stop Comparing Yourself to Others: Social media makes this even harder. It's easy to scroll through Instagram or Facebook and feel like everyone else has it all together. But here's the reality: social media is a highlight reel. People show their best moments, not their failures.

Focus on your own growth and stop comparing yourself to others. Your path is unique to you, and your imperfections are what make you, you.

5. Reframe Failure: Failure doesn't have to be a bad thing. In fact, failure is often the stepping stone to success. Every time you fail, you learn something new. Instead of fearing failure, embrace it. Reframe it as an opportunity to grow and improve. Remember, if you're not failing, you're probably not trying hard enough.

6. Set Realistic Expectations: Set goals that are challenging but achievable. Don't aim for perfection, but aim to improve and do your best. Perfectionism sets unrealistic standards that leave you feeling inadequate. Setting achievable, realistic expectations gives you a sense of accomplishment without overwhelming yourself.

7. Practice Self-Compassion: Be kind to yourself. When you make a mistake, treat yourself like you would treat a friend. Don't be your harshest critic. Offer yourself the same compassion and understanding you'd give someone else in the same situation.

The Power of Imperfections

Now, let me leave you with this: your imperfections are your superpower. They make you human. They allow you to connect with others on a deeper level because we all have flaws. We all make mistakes. And guess what? That's what makes life interesting.

If everything were perfect, life would be boring. It's the messiness, the struggles, and the imperfections that shape us and teach us valuable lessons. They challenge us, make us stronger, and inspire us to be better.

So, next time you feel scared of being imperfect, remember: embrace it. Don't hide your flaws. Don't run away from them. Because it's those very imperfections that can lead to something extraordinary.

Why Start from Today

Have you ever found yourself saying, "I'll start tomorrow"? It's almost like a habit, isn't it? We always believe that tomorrow will be the best time to begin something new—whether it's a new workout routine, a study plan, or pursuing a dream that's been on your mind for years. But here's the thing—tomorrow never really comes.

You see, today is the only time you can actually control. The future is uncertain, and the past is gone. So, why are we always putting things off for a better day that might never arrive?

Let's break down why starting today is so important, why procrastination is such a dangerous habit, and how making today the starting point can change your life.

The Power of Now

Let's be real for a second: how many of us have said we'd start something important tomorrow and ended up waiting until weeks, months, or even years have passed? It's easy to push things off because starting requires effort, and effort requires commitment. But here's the catch—procrastination kills progress.

There's a reason why people who take action today, rather than waiting for the perfect moment, often end up more successful. Every moment you waste waiting for the "right time" or the "perfect day" is time that could have been spent working toward your goal. The reality is, if you keep waiting for tomorrow, you're never going to get anywhere.

Why do you think they say "The best time to plant a tree was 20 years ago; the second-best time is now"? It's because today is the only moment you have the power to impact. You don't know if you'll have the same energy, motivation, or time tomorrow. So, why not use what you have now? Today is your opportunity—it's the one thing you can truly control.

Tomorrow Is Not Guaranteed

Let's take a step back for a second. What's one thing we know for sure? That we don't know what tomorrow will bring. Life can throw us curveballs. Things change unexpectedly. People move, jobs change, and health can fluctuate. The point is, tomorrow is never guaranteed.

If you've been putting something off for weeks or months because you were waiting for the perfect day to start, you've probably already wasted precious time. And who knows—maybe tomorrow something unexpected will happen that stops you from starting. Whether it's an emergency, a shift in your priorities, or just life getting in the way, you can't wait for tomorrow because tomorrow is a promise that may never come.

This isn't meant to sound morbid or pessimistic—it's just the reality. The only moment you can count on is the present. So, why waste it?

The Myth of Perfectionism

One of the main reasons people delay starting is the idea that they need to do everything perfectly. Let me tell you something: perfection is an illusion. There's no such thing as a perfect day to begin a project, a perfect moment to launch your career, or a perfect time to get fit. If you keep waiting for the "perfect" scenario, you'll be waiting forever.

Take a moment to think about it. How many times have you delayed something because it didn't feel like the right time? Maybe you didn't have the right equipment, the right space, or the right mindset. You told yourself, "Once I get this, I'll start." But that's the trap—perfectionism doesn't lead to success. Action does.

The key is to start imperfectly. Don't wait for everything to be in place. Take small steps forward, and trust me, you'll learn along the way. The first step is always the hardest, but once you start, things will get easier. Progress is built through action, not by waiting for things to fall into place.

Why Starting Today Creates Momentum

Here's something powerful about starting today: it creates momentum. The longer you wait to start, the harder it gets to take that first step. But once you start, even in the smallest way, you begin to build momentum. It's like a snowball rolling downhill—it starts small, but as it continues, it picks up speed and becomes more powerful.

The key to building momentum is to simply start. Action creates energy. You don't need to have everything figured out before you begin. You just need to take that first step. Once you've done that, the next step will seem easier, and the one after that even easier. Small actions lead to big results over time.

The hardest part isn't the journey itself; it's overcoming that mental barrier of "starting." Once you get past that, things start falling into place.

The Cost of Waiting

Let's talk about the price you pay for waiting. When you don't act today, you're not just losing time. You're losing opportunities. You're also losing out on growth. Think about how many things you could have accomplished by now if you'd started earlier—whether it's in your career, health, relationships, or personal growth. The longer you wait, the more you're delaying your own progress.

In the end, the cost of waiting is much higher than the discomfort of starting. Sure, starting may feel challenging, and maybe you won't have all the answers, but not starting guarantees that nothing will happen.

And don't you deserve to give yourself the chance to succeed? Don't you deserve to see how far you can go if you just take that first step? The cost of waiting isn't just about losing time; it's about losing the opportunity to become better.

What Happens When You Start Today

When you start today, everything changes. You'll start seeing things in a new light. Even if things don't go perfectly (spoiler: they won't), you'll learn more than you ever would have by just sitting around and waiting. Starting today means you're putting yourself in the game. You're no longer sitting on the sidelines, thinking about what could be; you're now actively creating what will be.

Here's the best part: the more you start today, the easier it gets. Starting becomes a habit, and once it's a habit, it becomes natural. You stop overthinking, stop procrastinating, and just do. And that's when real transformation begins.

Every little step you take today builds the foundation for your future success. It's not about jumping straight to your goals. It's about taking consistent action every day and staying committed, no matter how small the steps.

The Power of Small Starts

It's easy to feel overwhelmed by big goals, and that's another reason we put things off. But here's the thing: you don't need to do everything at once. Start small. Set manageable, bite-sized goals. Focus on today, not tomorrow. Even if your progress is small, it's still progress, and that counts.

You don't need to have everything figured out right now. It's okay to be uncertain, and it's okay to not know all the answers. What matters is that you're moving forward, even if it's just a little bit each day.

Think about a huge project you've been wanting to start—writing a book, learning a new skill, or even changing your lifestyle. It's easy to feel overwhelmed by the enormity of it. But, if you break it down and take the first step today, you'll be surprised at how quickly it starts adding up. One small effort today is far better than waiting for the "perfect moment" that might never come.

Conclusion: Today is Your Day

To sum it up: why wait for tomorrow? Starting today isn't just a good idea—it's the only option if you want to make progress. Tomorrow is an unknown. The future is a mystery. But today? Today is where the magic happens.

You can't control the past, and you can't predict the future, but you have the power to act today. You don't need to wait for a perfect moment, for all the stars to align, or for everything to be just right. Start where you are, use what you have, and do what you can.

Don't wait. Start today.

Self Discipline

Imagine waking up at 5 AM, hitting the gym, following a strict diet, finishing all your work on time, and still having enough energy to spend quality time with your loved ones. Sounds like a dream, right? But here's the thing: this can be your reality if you master self-discipline. It's the backbone of success and the key to achieving anything you set your mind to.

Let's take a deep dive into what self-discipline really is, why it's important, and how you can develop it in your own life. No fancy theories, just practical, real-life insights on how to make self-discipline work for you.

What is Self-Discipline?

Self-discipline, in simple terms, is the ability to control your emotions, behavior, and actions in the face of temptations and distractions. It's the art of doing what you need to do, even when you don't feel like it. Let me tell you—it's not about depriving yourself or making life miserable. It's about having the power to prioritize your long-term goals over short-term pleasures.

Now, I'm not talking about perfection here. We all slip up sometimes, and that's okay. The goal is progress, not perfection. Self-discipline means you stay focused on what really matters, even when it's hard. It's about consistency and commitment to your goals.

Why is Self-Discipline So Important?

Let's talk about why self-discipline is a game-changer. Have you ever found yourself procrastinating on something important, knowing you should be doing it, but just not able to push yourself to get started? Yeah, we've all been there. The issue here is that lack of self-discipline is the biggest reason why so many people fail to reach their potential.

Without self-discipline, it's too easy to get sidetracked by distractions. You know, Netflix episodes that turn into 6 hours of binge-watching, or that extra slice of cake when you're trying to stay healthy. These short-term rewards feel amazing in the moment, but what about your long-term dreams? They start slipping away bit by bit.

But, with self-discipline, you can overcome these temptations. It's not about never having fun or enjoying life; it's about knowing when to focus and when to indulge. Self-discipline is the bridge between where you are and where you want to be.

How to Build Self-Discipline?

Building self-discipline isn't an overnight thing. It takes time, effort, and a lot of small steps. But don't worry, I'll walk you through how to make it a part of your everyday life.

1. Start Small

Rome wasn't built in a day, and neither is self-discipline. If you're someone who struggles with sticking to tasks, don't dive straight into massive goals. Start small and build your way up.

For example, if you want to start exercising, don't commit to an hour every day right away. Start with just 10 minutes a day. Then, as you get used to it, gradually increase the time. Small wins lead to bigger successes.

2. Create a Routine

One of the best ways to stay disciplined is to create a routine. If you start your day with a set routine, it becomes much easier to stay focused and productive. You're setting up your mind to expect specific actions at specific times, and it builds discipline over time.

For instance, wake up at the same time every day, plan your meals, block time for work, and make sure you follow through. Routine creates a sense of responsibility and helps you develop self-discipline naturally.

3. Remove Temptations

Let's be honest, temptations are everywhere. Whether it's social media, junk food, or that never-ending to-do list, distractions can throw you off course in seconds. But with self-discipline, you have to learn to eliminate distractions, or at least reduce them.

Take your phone, for example. If you know that scrolling through Instagram eats up an hour of your day, put it out of reach while you work. Or turn off your notifications to stay focused. The key is creating an environment that supports your goals, not one that sabotages them.

4. Focus on Your 'Why'

One of the easiest ways to stay disciplined is by constantly reminding yourself why you're doing something. Why do you want to get fit? Why do you want to study harder? Why do you want to start a business?

Your "why" will serve as your driving force, especially when things get tough. When you feel like quitting, remembering your reason for starting can keep you going. And let's face it, you're much more likely to push through the challenges if you have a strong reason to do so.

5. Be Accountable

Accountability is a huge factor in building self-discipline. Tell someone about your goals. It could be a friend, a family member, or even an online community. When you have someone to answer to, it's harder to slack off. Accountability gives you an extra layer of motivation.

You could also keep a journal to track your progress. Write down what you did well and where you need improvement. This will not only hold you accountable but also allow you to see your growth over time.

6. Learn to Say 'No'

If you want to build self-discipline, you need to learn the power of saying no. It's so easy to get distracted by other people's needs, social invitations, or things that don't align with your goals. But every time you say yes to something that doesn't serve your vision, you're saying no to your own dreams.

Get comfortable with saying "no" to things that don't add value to your life. It's not being rude; it's being disciplined about what's most important to you.

7. Embrace Failure as Part of the Process

Building self-discipline isn't about being perfect; it's about persistence. Failure is a part of success. The key is to learn from your mistakes and not let them derail your progress. Don't be too hard on yourself if you slip up. The important thing is to get back on track and keep moving forward.

Benefits of Self-Discipline

You might be wondering, "Okay, this sounds great, but what's in it for me?" Well, let me tell you—self-discipline doesn't just help you stay on track, it also improves every area of your life. Here's how:

1. More Productivity

When you're disciplined, you spend less time procrastinating and more time getting things done. You stop wasting time on irrelevant tasks and focus on what really matters. This leads to greater productivity, and the more productive you are, the more you'll achieve.

2. Improved Mental Health

Believe it or not, being disciplined helps reduce anxiety. When you know you're making progress, even if it's small, you feel more confident. You have a sense of control, and that can lead to a positive mindset.

3. Greater Success

Self-discipline is directly linked to success. People who master self-discipline consistently achieve their goals because they take action every single day, even when they don't feel like it. That's how success is built—by sticking to your goals, no matter how tough things get.

4. More Free Time

This might sound contradictory, but hear me out: when you're disciplined, you get things done faster. By staying focused and following through, you're more efficient with your time. This means you can enjoy more free time for yourself, without the stress of unfinished tasks hanging over your head.

Conclusion: Discipline is Freedom

Self-discipline isn't about being strict with yourself or living a life of restriction. It's about creating habits that allow you to live the life you want. Discipline is freedom—freedom to pursue your goals, freedom to enjoy your time, and freedom to become the best version of yourself.

It all starts with small steps. By practicing self-discipline today, you set yourself up for success tomorrow. Don't wait for the "perfect" moment. Start with whatever you can, wherever you are. And remember, discipline isn't a one-time thing—it's a lifelong habit.

"Your Move:"

What's one thing you've been delaying? Write it down.

Now, take one small action toward it. Not tomorrow, right now.

Are you ready? Then go.

II

STOP PLANNING START DOING

Alright, let's be honest—how many times have you planned something so perfectly in your head that it felt like you had already achieved it? Hmm? Be real. You imagined yourself waking up at 5 AM, hitting the gym, eating healthy, working like a productivity beast, and BOOM—your life is transformed. Hahaha, sounds like a dream, right? But here's the thing—you never actually did it.

Oh shit.

See, that's the illusion of perfect planning. We love making perfect plans. We sit there, thinking, brainstorming, creating the most detailed strategies. We feel productive, we feel like we're making progress. But in reality? We're just tricking ourselves.

The Trap of Overplanning

Planning is important, no doubt. But planning can also be a trap. You know why? Because it makes you feel like you're working when you're actually doing nothing.

Think about it—how many times have you spent hours researching, watching productivity videos, making to-do lists, buying planners, and setting reminders... but when the time comes to actually start? You suddenly feel tired. Dam it.

Why does this happen?

Because planning gives you dopamine—the same chemical that makes you feel happy when you accomplish something. The moment you make a perfect plan, your brain goes, "Wow! We did something amazing!" But in reality, you haven't moved a single inch.

It's like imagining yourself running a marathon, sweating, pushing through pain, crossing the finish line—and then just sitting on your couch eating chips. Hahaha, what a joke, right? But that's exactly what happens when we overplan and under-execute.

The Fear Behind Perfection

Let's dig a little deeper. Why do we love perfect planning so much?

One word—fear.

Fear of failure, fear of making mistakes, fear of not being good enough. So, instead of taking action, we hide behind planning. We tell ourselves, "I'll start when everything is perfect." But perfect never comes.

Listen, mistakes are going to happen. You're going to mess up. So what? That's how you learn.

Remember your first time riding a bicycle? Did you sit there making a step-by-step plan for months? No! You just hopped on, fell a few times, and learned. But now, as adults, we act like we need a NASA-level strategy to start even the smallest thing.

Wow, how smart we've become. (Sarcasm intended.)

Action Beats Perfection Every Time

Here's the truth—a half-baked, imperfect action is better than a perfect plan that never happens.

Let's take two people:

1. John, the planner: Spends months creating the "perfect" business plan, researching every little detail, waiting for the "right time."

2. Mike, the doer: Starts immediately, makes mistakes, learns, adapts, and improves as he goes.

Fast forward one year—who do you think is ahead? Mike. Every single time.

Because here's a simple rule of life: You cannot improve something you haven't even started.

Oh, you want to start a YouTube channel? Just make your first video. It will suck, and that's okay. You'll get better.

Want to hit the gym? Stop waiting for the "perfect workout plan" and just show up.

Want to write a book? Open a blank document and start typing. Even if the first draft is garbage, it's still better than an empty page.

How to Break the Illusion of Perfect Planning

Alright, enough talk. Now, let's get real. How do you actually break free from this trap?

1. Set a Deadline for Planning

Give yourself a time limit for planning. Need to start a project? Fine, take a day to plan. But once the deadline is up—start. No excuses.

2. Follow the "2-Minute Rule"

If something takes less than 2 minutes, do it NOW. Stop adding tiny tasks to your endless "perfect plan" list. Just get it done.

3. Start Before You're Ready

You will never feel 100% ready. So stop waiting for the "right moment." Start messy. Start uncomfortable. Just start.

4. Track Action, Not Just Plans

Instead of feeling good about planning, start feeling good about taking action. Keep a journal of what you did, not what you planned.

5. Embrace Failure as a Teacher

Every mistake is a lesson. Every failure is a step forward. Instead of fearing it, use it to grow.

Final Thoughts

Look, I get it. We all love making plans. It's fun. It's safe. It makes us feel like we're doing something. But if all you do is plan, and never execute—you're just fooling yourself.

So, enough with the perfect plans. It's time to get your hands dirty.

Hahaha, you know what? Just stop reading now and go do something. Anything. Even if it's small. Just start.

Because done is always better than perfect.

Analysis Paralysis: When Thinking Too Much Kills Action

Alright, let's talk about something that messes up more dreams than bad luck or lack of talent ever could—overthinking. You know that feeling when you want to do something, but instead of just doing it, your brain turns into a crime scene investigation unit? Yeah, that's analysis paralysis.

It's like you're standing at the edge of a swimming pool, thinking about jumping in. But instead of diving, you start analyzing—How cold is the water? What if I slip? What if I don't swim properly? What if someone laughs at me? And while you're lost in these thoughts, someone else just jumps in, enjoys the swim, and moves on with life. Damn it, right?

Why Do We Overthink?

Let's be real, overthinking feels kinda smart. It tricks us into believing that we're being "careful" or "well-prepared." But in reality, we're just stuck. It's like buffering on a slow internet connection. Annoying, frustrating, and absolutely useless.

Here's why we do it:

1. Fear of Failure – "What if I mess up?" Bro, what if you succeed?

2. Desire for Perfection – "I need the perfect plan." Newsflash: No plan is ever perfect.

3. Too Many Choices – Ever spent 30 minutes scrolling Netflix, only to end up watching nothing? Yeah, that.

4. Seeking Approval – We worry too much about what others will think. Spoiler: They don't care.

The Illusion of the 'Perfect Plan'

One of the biggest traps of overthinking is waiting for the "perfect moment" or the "perfect plan." Guess what? That moment doesn't exist. If it did, everyone would be successful already. The truth? You learn by doing.

Imagine you're planning to start a YouTube channel. You spend months researching the best camera, best microphone, best editing software. Meanwhile, some random guy with a shaky phone camera is already getting thousands of views because he just started.

Planning is important, but too much planning becomes an excuse for not starting.

Action Beats Overthinking Every Time

Look, I get it. You want things to go smoothly. You don't want to make mistakes. But let me hit you with a truth bomb—mistakes are inevitable. If you're waiting for a mistake-free path, you'll be waiting forever.

Think about babies learning to walk. Do they sit there, thinking, "Hmm, let me analyze the physics of walking before I take my first step." Nope. They just stand up, fall, get back up, and eventually, they're running all over the place. That's how you win at life—by doing.

The 'Thinking vs. Doing' Ratio

A simple rule: If you're thinking 80% of the time and doing only 20%, you're stuck. Flip the ratio. Think 20%, do 80%. That's how things get done. Successful people don't sit around analyzing every little detail; they take action, adjust along the way, and keep moving.

Want to write a book? Start writing. Want to get fit? Hit the gym. Want to start a business? Launch something small today. Start messy. Improve later.

How to Break Free from Analysis Paralysis

So, how do we stop overthinking and start doing? Here are some battle-tested strategies:

1. Set a Deadline for Decisions – Give yourself a time limit. "I'll decide by tonight and act tomorrow." No extensions!

2. Use the 'Two-Minute Rule' – If something takes less than two minutes, do it immediately. No overthinking.

3. Limit Your Choices – Fewer options = faster decisions. Instead of reading 50 articles about the best diet, pick one and stick to it.

4. Accept Imperfection – Understand that your first attempt will suck. That's fine. Done is better than perfect.

5. Ask Yourself: What's the Worst That Can Happen? – Most of the time, the worst-case scenario isn't even that bad.

6. Take Small Steps – Overwhelmed? Break your goal into tiny steps. Instead of "I need to launch a business," say, "I need to create a simple website today."

7. Act First, Think Later – Sometimes, the best way to make a decision is to just start and adjust on the go.

Real-Life Example: The 'Overthinking vs. Action' Experiment

Let me tell you about two people I know.

Person A wanted to start a podcast. He spent months researching, buying the best mic, learning editing software, reading about "how to grow a podcast." But guess what? He never actually started.

Person B? He just picked up his phone, recorded his thoughts, and uploaded them. Was it perfect? Hell no. But he kept improving. Fast forward a year—he now has thousands of listeners.

See the difference? One was stuck in analysis paralysis. The other took action.

Final Thought: Action Creates Clarity

Here's the ultimate hack: Clarity comes from action, not from thinking. The more you do, the more you learn. The more you learn, the better you get.

If you've been waiting for a sign to start that thing you've been overthinking, THIS IS IT.

Stop thinking. Start doing. Because at the end of the day, overthinking doesn't take you anywhere—action does.

Now go make it happen!

The 24-Hour Rule: Execute First, Refine Later

Alright, let's be real. How many times have you had a great idea, got super excited about it, and then... never actually did anything about it? Hmm? Be honest. Maybe you planned it, maybe you wrote it down, maybe you even told your friends about it—but somehow, it just never happened.

Welcome to the world of overthinking, where ideas go to die. Damm it.

But what if I told you that the solution to this neverending cycle of procrastination is something ridiculously simple? Something that could actually change your entire approach to productivity? It's called the 24-Hour Rule.

What is the 24-Hour Rule?

It's simple: The moment you get an idea or a task, take action on it within 24 hours—no excuses.

Action doesn't mean you have to complete the whole thing in a day. It just means you need to start. Even if it's just a tiny step. The goal? To stop overthinking and start moving.

Because let's be honest, once you start something, the momentum kicks in. And when momentum kicks in, magic happens. Wow.

Why is This Rule So Powerful?

1. Kills Overthinking Before It Kills You Thinking is great. Overthinking? Not so much. If you give yourself too much time before starting, your brain will start throwing doubts at you. "Is this even a good idea? What if it fails? What if I'm not good enough?" Oh shit. Here we go again.

The 24-Hour Rule shuts that nonsense down. You don't give yourself time to question whether or not you should do something. You just start.

2. Builds the Habit of Immediate Action The more you delay things, the more you train your brain that "it's okay to wait." But when you take action immediately, even in small ways, you train yourself to be an action-taker. And let's be real, action-takers are the ones who get things done. Not the dreamers, not the planners, but the doers.

3. Removes the Need for Perfection Perfection is a myth. Hahaha. You think you'll get it perfect the first time? Nope. And guess what? That's completely fine. The 24-Hour Rule forces you to just start, knowing that you can refine, fix, or improve things later. Because action beats perfection every single time.

How to Apply the 24-Hour Rule in Your Life

Okay, now that we know why this works, let's get into the "how." Because, let's be real, you're probably thinking, "Sounds great, but how do I actually do this?" Don't worry, I got you.

1. Write Down the Idea Immediately

Your brain is a messy place. Thoughts come, thoughts go. If you don't capture them, they're gone forever. Write it down. Right now. Use a notebook, your phone, a napkin—whatever. Just make sure you don't let the idea slip away.

2. Take One Small Action Within 24 Hours

This is the golden rule. You don't have to do the whole thing, but you must do something.

If you want to start a YouTube channel, film a 10-second video.

If you want to write a book, draft the first paragraph.

If you want to start a fitness journey, do 5 push-ups right now.

If you want to start a business, create a basic logo or brainstorm your first product.

The goal is not to be perfect. The goal is just to start.

3. Forget About "Perfect Conditions"

There is no perfect time. There is no perfect setup. There is no perfect mindset. The biggest lie we tell ourselves is "I'll start when the time is right." Bruh. The time will never be right. You just gotta do it anyway.

4. Embrace the "Messy First Draft" Mentality

Your first attempt will suck. Accept it. Love it. Laugh at it. But whatever you do, don't let it stop you. Because once you have something—anything—you can improve it. But if you don't start, you have nothing to improve.

5. Set a Deadline and Stick to It

You know how you always get things done at the last minute? That's because deadlines force action. Use that to your advantage. Give yourself a deadline, even if it's artificial. If you say, "I have to get this done by tomorrow night," you'll actually move.

6. Tell Someone About It

Accountability is a powerful thing. Tell a friend, a sibling, or even post it on social media. Once you say it out loud, you create a sense of commitment. And when people ask you about it later, you'll have to admit whether you did it or not.

Real-Life Examples of the 24-Hour Rule

Still not convinced? Alright, let's look at some real examples.

YouTube Creators – Ever noticed how new YouTubers always say, "I was scared to start, but I just decided to post my first video, and now here we are?" That's the 24-Hour Rule in action. The hardest part is the first upload.

Writers – Every famous author was once a nobody with a blank page. They didn't write a bestseller in a day. They wrote something in a day, then improved it over time.

Entrepreneurs – Jeff Bezos didn't start Amazon with a perfect business plan. He just started selling books online and figured things out along the way.

What Happens If You Don't Follow This Rule?

Well... nothing. And that's the problem. If you don't take action, nothing happens.

Your ideas stay ideas. Your dreams stay dreams. Your goals stay goals. You stay stuck in the same place, watching others move forward while you keep "thinking" about it. Damn. That's a tough pill to swallow. But hey, it's the truth.

Final Thoughts

Listen. The difference between successful people and everyone else isn't intelligence, luck, or talent. It's action. The ones who win in life are the ones who take action, even when they don't feel ready. Especially when they don't feel ready.

So, next time you get an idea, don't sit on it. Don't overthink it. Don't wait for the perfect moment. Use the 24-Hour Rule. Start something. Anything.

Because action today is better than a perfect plan tomorrow. And if you keep waiting for "someday," you'll wake up one day and realize that someday never came.

Now go. Take action. Within the next 24 hours. No excuses.

I believe in you. Now believe in yourself.

Let's get it. Hahaha.

Fail Fast, Learn Faster

Alright, let's get real. We all want to succeed, right? But here's the thing—nobody, and I mean NOBODY, figures it all out on their first try. That's where the magic of failing fast comes in. The faster you fail, the quicker you learn. And the quicker you learn, the faster you win. Simple? Hmm, maybe not. But let's break it down in a way that actually makes sense.

The Fear of Failing(*Oh shit, what if I mess up?*)

Failure sucks. Nobody wants to look dumb, make mistakes, or feel like they wasted time. But the truth? Failure is not the opposite of success. It's part of success. Every mistake teaches you something. Every wrong move shows you the right one. And if you keep delaying action just because you're scared to fail, you'll NEVER get anywhere.

Think about learning how to ride a bike. Did you master it on the first try? Nope. You fell, scraped your knee, maybe even cried a little. But then you got back up, tried again, and boom! One day, you were cruising like a pro. Life works the same way.

The "Perfect Time" is a Lie

Let me tell you a secret: There is no perfect time to start. Waiting for the stars to align? For your skills to be 100% ready? For the "right" moment? Hahaha, keep waiting, and you'll be stuck forever. The people who succeed aren't the ones who had perfect timing. They're the ones who started even when they weren't ready.

Successful people fail faster because they take action NOW. They don't waste time overthinking. They jump in, make mistakes, fix them, and move forward. Meanwhile, overthinkers are still sitting in their rooms, planning, analyzing, and doubting themselves.

Fail Faster, But Smartly

Okay, let's be real. I'm not saying go out and make stupid mistakes just for the sake of failing. There's a way to fail smartly—

1. Start Small: If you're trying something new, don't go all in without testing. Dip your toes in, mess up a little, learn, and adjust.

2. Fail Cheaply: If you're testing an idea, don't spend all your money on it right away. Try a small version, see what happens, and then expand.

3. Learn Every Time: The biggest mistake? Making the same mistake twice. Fail fast, but don't fail the same way again. Take notes, improve, and level up.

4. Don't Take It Personally: Failing doesn't mean YOU are a failure. It just means you tried something that didn't work. Keep going.

Action > Regret

Imagine looking back 10 years from now, thinking about all the things you WANTED to do but never did. Ouch. That's a painful thought, right? Would you rather fail and learn, or never try and regret it forever?

Failing fast isn't about being reckless. It's about being fearless. It's about trusting yourself enough to take risks, knowing that every mistake brings you one step closer to success.

So, what's stopping you? Go fail at something today, and learn faster than ever. You got this!

Why Execution is the Ultimate Teacher

Hey buddy! Let's get real for a second. How many times have you spent hours, days, or even weeks just thinking about doing something, only to never actually do it? We all do it. We plan, we analyze, we try to perfect our strategy before taking action. But here's the cold, hard truth—no amount of planning can replace actual execution. You don't truly learn by thinking; you learn by doing.

The Trap of Overthinking

We often believe that if we just think a little longer, plan a little better, or prepare a little more, we'll be ready to take action. But guess what? That moment never comes. Hahaha, dam it! We keep waiting for the "perfect time," but it doesn't exist. The only real way to figure things out is by starting.

Have you ever tried learning to swim by watching YouTube videos? Oh shit, that's a disaster waiting to happen! You can understand the strokes, breathing techniques, and perfect posture, but the second you hit the water, everything changes. Suddenly, your body doesn't move the way you imagined, and you realize you have no idea what you're doing. That's because real learning happens in action, not in theory.

Why Execution is the Best Teacher

1. You Learn Faster – Imagine two people trying to start a business. One spends a year researching, making business plans, and calculating risks. The other just starts selling something and learns from mistakes along the way. Who do you think will succeed faster? The one who took action. Because experience teaches lessons that no book, video, or course ever can.

2. Mistakes Give Real Insights – Let's say you want to be a stand-up comedian. You can watch all the greats, analyze their jokes, and rehearse in front of the mirror. But the first time you perform live? Boom! You forget your lines, the audience doesn't laugh, and you feel embarrassed. However, that's exactly what teaches you which jokes land, what doesn't work, and how to improve. No amount of theory can prepare you for the real deal.

3. Confidence Comes from Doing – Have you noticed how nervous you feel before trying something new? But once you've done it a few times, it's like second nature? That's because confidence doesn't come from planning; it comes from experience. The first time you ride a bike, you're terrified. But after falling a few times, you suddenly get the hang of it. That's execution in action!

The Execution vs. Knowledge Gap

There's a massive gap between knowing and doing. You might know exactly how to lose weight—eat healthy, exercise, stay consistent. But unless you actually do it, nothing changes. Knowledge is useless without execution.

Think about all those people who read self-help books but never apply what they learn. They know everything about success but never actually achieve anything. Why? Because they're stuck in the cycle of learning without action. Hahaha, it's like buying a gym membership and thinking that alone will get you fit. Nope, buddy, you gotta show up and do the work!

How to Shift from Thinking to Doing

1. Start Before You Feel Ready – If you wait to feel fully prepared, you'll never start. Jump in, make mistakes, and learn on the go.

2. Set a Deadline for Learning – Give yourself a strict time limit for research. After that, take action no matter what.

3. Embrace Failure as a Lesson – Stop seeing failure as a stop sign. Instead, treat it as a teacher. Each mistake is one step closer to mastery.

4. Take Small Steps Every Day – Even tiny actions count. If you want to write a book, start with one paragraph a day. If you want to start a business, sell one product. Small steps lead to big results.

5. Surround Yourself with Action-Takers – If you hang out with people who only talk but never do, you'll stay stuck. Find people who take action, and their energy will push you forward.

Conclusion

Look, buddy, the ultimate truth is simple—execution beats perfection every single time. You don't need the perfect plan, the perfect moment, or perfect knowledge. What you need is to start. The real lessons are in the doing. So whatever you've been thinking about starting—whether it's a fitness goal, a new skill, or a life-changing decision—just go for it.

No more waiting. No more excuses. It's time to execute!

Now tell me, what's that one thing you've been delaying? Let's get it done! Hmm, wow, I can alre

Momentum vs Motivation: Which One Really Moves You?

Hey, let's have a little heart-to-heart. So many of us are constantly searching for motivation, right? We think that the moment we get that "spark" of motivation, we'll start crushing our goals, and everything will fall into place. But what if I told you that motivation isn't the real key? In fact, it's not even the thing that will help you push through when things get tough. What truly drives long-term success is something a bit more consistent: momentum. Sounds a bit weird, right? Let me explain.

Motivation – The Initial Spark

We've all been there. You wake up one morning feeling like a champion, ready to tackle everything on your to-do list. You feel motivated, fired up, and ready to take on the world. It's like someone just injected you with a shot of energy. And that's great! Motivation is the thing that gets you moving. Without it, you'd probably never get out of bed, start that new project, or go after that dream.

But, here's the catch—motivation doesn't last. It's like that sugar rush you get after eating your favorite candy. You feel great for a while, but before you know it, the sugar high crashes, and you're back to square one, feeling lazy and unproductive. Hahaha, sound familiar?

We often rely on motivation to keep us going, but it's really not something you can count on. It's temporary, fleeting, and can leave you hanging when you need it the most. That's where momentum comes in.

Momentum – The Power of Consistency

Here's the magic sauce: momentum. Unlike motivation, momentum doesn't come and go based on how you feel that day. Momentum is built over time. It's the snowball effect—the more you do, the more you can do.

Think of momentum like this: You're pushing a heavy rock up a hill. In the beginning, it's hard as hell. Every little push feels like it's draining you. But if you keep pushing, keep making progress, that rock starts rolling downhill on its own. It gains speed, and soon it feels like you're not even doing that much. The work you put in early on creates the energy that keeps the ball rolling. The same thing happens with habits, productivity, and even your goals.

Momentum doesn't care about motivation. It's about taking small actions consistently, even when you don't feel like it. And before you know it, those actions compound and create the results you've been working for. It's not about one huge push; it's about a series of small, consistent efforts.

Why Motivation Fades but Momentum Builds

Here's the simple truth: motivation is about feeling, while momentum is about action. Motivation comes from an emotional place, and emotions are all over the place. Some days you feel on top of the world, and other days, you just don't feel like it. On the flip side, momentum is created by doing. It's built by getting started—even if you don't feel like it. It's like riding a bike: once you start pedaling, it becomes easier to keep going.

Example: The Gym Struggle

Let's say you're trying to get into a fitness routine. You wake up on a Monday morning, and BAM—you're motivated. You hit the gym, crush your workout, feel awesome, and can't wait to do it again. But by Wednesday, that motivation starts to fade. You're tired, your muscles hurt, and all you want to do is stay in bed. You start to make excuses, thinking, "Maybe I'll go tomorrow." Sound familiar?

This is where momentum steps in. The first few workouts were hard, right? But if you can push through, even when you don't feel like it, you'll start to notice something amazing—you'll start to feel the momentum building. Your body adapts, you get stronger, and your workouts start to feel easier. And once you hit that momentum, it's harder to stop. It's like your body and mind are in sync, and you just keep going. Momentum keeps you in the game, even when motivation has left the building.

How to Build Momentum (Even Without Motivation)

Okay, so now you're probably wondering, "How the heck do I build momentum when I don't feel motivated?" Don't worry, I got you covered. The good news is, momentum can be built even when motivation is nowhere in sight. Here's how:

1. Start Small

When you're not feeling motivated, the last thing you want to do is tackle a huge task. Instead, start with small, manageable steps. If you want to write a book, don't aim for 3 chapters on the first day. Start with 100 words. If you want to get fit, don't aim for a full gym session; just go for a 10-minute walk. Small actions like these might seem insignificant at first, but over time, they create momentum. Slowly, those small steps will turn into big actions.

2. Set Non-Negotiable Routines

One of the most powerful ways to build momentum is to create non-negotiable routines. Think of them like habits that you commit to no matter what. Maybe it's writing for 15 minutes every morning or doing 5 push-ups every day. Whatever it is, make it something that you can do without fail. Routines eliminate the need for motivation because they become automatic. And when you stick to your routine, you'll start to build momentum.

3. Don't Wait for Perfection

Waiting for the "perfect" time, mood, or setup is a trap. Momentum doesn't need perfection; it needs action. Start with what you've got, even if you don't have all the answers.

As you keep moving, you'll learn, improve, and adjust. The key is to take that first step. Trust me, once you do, you'll be surprised at how quickly momentum builds.

4. Track Your Progress

Tracking your progress is a great way to stay motivated and keep your momentum going. Whether it's crossing items off a to-do list, keeping a journal, or using an app to track your goals, seeing your progress builds confidence and fuels your momentum.

5. Celebrate Small Wins

Every time you complete a small task or reach a milestone, take a moment to celebrate. Those small wins are the fuel that keeps the momentum going. So, whether it's treating yourself to a coffee, taking a break, or just acknowledging your success, don't forget to celebrate your progress.

Motivation vs. Momentum: The Big Takeaway

Let's wrap it up, shall we? Motivation is amazing when it's there, but it's unpredictable. It can fade just as quickly as it arrives. Momentum, on the other hand, is built through consistent action. It doesn't need motivation to thrive; it thrives because of action. And once you've built momentum, it becomes a lot easier to keep going.

So, next time you're stuck in the cycle of waiting for motivation to kick in, remember this: start small, stay consistent, and focus on building momentum. Over time, that momentum will propel you forward—whether or not you feel motivated. That's the secret to long-term success.

Now go ahead, take that first step, and let momentum take care of the rest. Hmm, wow, can already see you getting things done!

The Just 5 Minutes Trick: How Small Actions Lead to Big Results

Sometimes, the biggest barrier to achieving your goals isn't the task itself but getting started. We've all been there: staring at a mountain of work, feeling overwhelmed, and thinking, "There's no way I can get all this done." So, what do we do? We procrastinate. We find other things to do, check social media, or just put it off for "later."

But what if I told you that you could defeat procrastination with just five minutes? Yes, you heard me right—five minutes. Trust me, this simple trick will change the way you approach your goals and tasks, no matter how big or small.

What's the Deal with the Just 5 Minutes Trick?

The Just 5 Minutes Trick is exactly what it sounds like. Instead of telling yourself that you need to work on something for hours, you simply commit to doing it for just five minutes. That's it. Five minutes might not seem like a lot of time, but that small time frame can trick your brain into getting started.

You see, often the hardest part of any task is getting started. Once you get over that initial resistance, things tend to flow more easily. But if you think of the whole task as one huge, overwhelming project, it's easy to feel paralyzed. That's where the Just 5 Minutes Trick comes in—it removes the pressure to do everything at once, making the task feel more manageable.

It's All About Breaking the Mental Block

When you tell yourself, "I'll work on this for just five minutes," you're breaking the mental block. It's kind of like when you're trying to get yourself to exercise. You tell yourself, "I'll just do a five-minute walk," and before you know it, you've been walking for 20 minutes. The key is that once you start, you've already broken through the hardest part.

The reason why this trick works is because it reduces the feeling of pressure. If you tell yourself you need to work for an hour or two, it can feel overwhelming, like the task is endless. But five minutes? That's doable. And when you start with small, easy steps, you gradually build momentum. You're more likely to continue once you've taken that first step.

The Power of Starting Small

Starting small is one of the most powerful ways to beat procrastination. Think about it—if you sit down to write an essay, you might feel paralyzed by the blank page. But when you commit to just writing for five minutes, you're giving yourself permission to take the pressure off. You're allowing yourself to get started without worrying about the end result.

Small steps add up. That's the magic behind the Just 5 Minutes Trick. Even though you're only committing to a small amount of time, you'll often find that once those five minutes are over, you're in the flow and ready to keep going. Five minutes turns into ten, and ten turns into twenty. Suddenly, you've completed a task that you were avoiding.

Why Five Minutes Works Better Than an Hour

It's easy to get stuck thinking that the longer you work on something, the better it will be. But here's the thing—quality over quantity. When you commit to working for just five minutes, you're less likely to feel mentally exhausted. Your brain isn't thinking about the "long haul," so it can focus on the task at hand.

When you think you need to work for an entire hour, it can feel overwhelming. It's like running a marathon in your head before you've even taken a single step. But when you commit to just five minutes, you're allowing yourself to ease into it, without the stress of thinking about how much time is left.

If you feel like you can't keep going after five minutes, that's okay. The point is, you've made a start. And that's a huge win! You can always come back to it later. But nine times out of ten, once those five minutes are over, you'll find that you're already into the task and don't want to stop.

Overcoming Perfectionism with the Just 5 Minutes Trick

Do you ever find yourself stuck in a loop of perfectionism, thinking that everything has to be perfect before you even begin? I know I've been there. You want to write the perfect email, create the perfect presentation, or cook the perfect meal. But perfectionism is just another form of procrastination.

The Just 5 Minutes Trick helps you overcome this by getting rid of the idea that everything has to be perfect from the start. When you commit to five minutes, you're telling yourself that it's okay to start imperfectly. That's the beauty of it—you give yourself permission to make mistakes, learn, and improve as you go.

Perfectionism can keep you stuck. It's paralyzing, because you're so focused on getting everything just right that you never take the first step. But five minutes is manageable. It's not enough time to get everything "perfect," and that's the point! Just focus on making progress, and you can refine things later.

The Just 5 Minutes Trick for Big Goals

Big goals can be intimidating. Whether it's writing a book, starting a business, or getting in shape, it's easy to get overwhelmed by the size of the task. But here's the secret—big goals are achieved through small, consistent actions. And the Just 5 Minutes Trick is the perfect way to start making progress toward those goals.

Let's say your goal is to write a book. Thinking about writing an entire book can feel like a mountain that you'll never climb. But if you commit to writing for just five minutes every day, you'll be surprised at how quickly the pages add up. After a week, you'll have 35 minutes of writing under your belt. After a month, you'll have 140 minutes—enough to make serious progress.

The same principle applies to any big goal. The key is not to get caught up in the enormity of the task. Focus on small, manageable actions. Commit to five minutes, and you'll be amazed at how those five minutes add up over time.

The Just 5 Minutes Trick for Breaking Bad Habits

The Just 5 Minutes Trick isn't just for starting good habits; it can also help you break bad ones. Let's say you want to quit smoking. It might feel impossible to stop, but what if you committed to resisting the urge for just five minutes? Those five minutes are the first small step toward breaking the habit.

Every time you resist that urge, you're building your ability to say no. And if you can do it for five minutes, you'll find it's easier to resist the next time. Over time, those five-minute victories turn into bigger successes, and eventually, you'll have successfully broken the bad habit.

The Psychology Behind the Just 5 Minutes Trick

So, why does this trick work? It all comes down to psychology. When we see a big task, our brains often signal a sense of overwhelm. This leads to procrastination because we're focused on the entire task rather than breaking it into smaller, more manageable pieces.

By committing to just five minutes, we're tricking our brains into thinking it's no big deal. It doesn't feel overwhelming, so we're more likely to start. The brain doesn't feel the same level of resistance because we're not thinking about the whole task. Plus, once we start, we get into the flow of things, and the five minutes often turn into longer periods of productivity.

How to Use the Just 5 Minutes Trick Effectively

To make the Just 5 Minutes Trick work for you, here are a few tips:

1. Set a Timer: Set a timer for five minutes, and focus solely on the task at hand. No distractions, no checking your phone. Just five minutes of pure focus.

2. Commit to Consistency: The more you use the trick, the easier it becomes. Make it a habit to start with five minutes, and soon it'll be second nature.

3. Celebrate Small Wins: After your five minutes are up, celebrate the fact that you got started. Even small wins deserve recognition.

The Bottom Line: It's All About Getting Started

The Just 5 Minutes Trick is all about taking that first step. It's easy to get stuck in the cycle of procrastination, but by committing to just five minutes, you can break free from that cycle. Five minutes might not seem like much, but it's enough to get you started—and once you start, it's much easier to keep going.

So, next time you're feeling overwhelmed or stuck, remember this: just five minutes. Set the timer, get started, and watch how those five minutes turn into big results.

Hmm, wow, can already see you making progress, huh? Keep it up!

"Your Move:"

What's one thing you've been overthinking instead of doing?

Take action right now—even if it's small.

Are you ready? Then stop thinking and start doing.
ady see you taking action!

III

FEAR WILL BE ALWAYS EXIST BUT SO WILL VICTORY

Fear Will Always Exist, but So Will Victory

Fear. Hmm. Just the word itself feels heavy, right? It's like this invisible force that creeps into your mind, making you doubt yourself, making you hesitate, making you wonder if you're really capable of doing what you want to do. Wow, that sounds dramatic, but dam it, it's true.

Now, here's the thing: Fear will always be there. No matter how strong you become, how successful you are, or how many battles you've fought, fear doesn't vanish. Oh shit, that sounds like bad news, doesn't it? But wait, here's the good part—victory always exists too. The key is not to get rid of fear but to act despite it. Hahaha, sounds simple, right? But we both know it's not.

Let's break this down.

The Nature of Fear

Fear isn't just something that happens to weak people. Even the strongest feel it. It's part of being human. The problem isn't fear itself; the problem is what you do when you feel it. Hmm, do you stop? Do you overthink? Do you let it paralyze you? Or do you push through? That's where the difference lies between those who win and those who don't.

Think about any major success story. Athletes, entrepreneurs, artists, leaders—every single one of them had fear. But they acted anyway. They didn't wait for the fear to disappear. Instead, they carried it with them, used it as fuel, and moved forward.

Why Fear Feels So Real

Fear tricks you. It makes things seem scarier than they are. Your brain goes into survival mode and exaggerates the danger. That's why something as simple as public speaking can feel like standing on the edge of a cliff. Your brain is trying to protect you, but dam it, sometimes it overreacts.

But here's a wild thought—what if you could use fear to your advantage? Instead of seeing it as a stop sign, what if you saw it as a green light? A sign that says, 'Hey, this is important! Go for it!' Hahaha, sounds crazy, right? But stay with me.

Fear vs. Victory: The Real Battle

Victory doesn't mean you're fearless. It means you acted despite fear. It means you didn't let fear control your choices. Every time you face fear and still move forward, you win. And every time you let fear stop you, fear wins.

Hmm, that's actually a pretty simple formula, isn't it?

Fear exists. That's a fact.

But so does victory.

The winner is the one you choose to feed.

Oh shit, that hit hard, didn't it?

The Fear of Imperfection

One of the biggest fears that stop people is the fear of imperfection. 'What if I mess up? What if I fail? What if people laugh at me?'

Newsflash: No one starts perfect. No one. Perfection is a myth. The sooner you accept that, the sooner you can start winning. Imagine if babies were afraid of falling. Would they ever learn to walk? Hahaha, can you picture a baby saying, 'No, I won't even try walking until I'm sure I won't fall'?

Sounds ridiculous, right? But that's exactly what we do as adults. We wait until we feel 'ready.' Until we feel 'perfect.' And guess what? That moment never comes.

Overthinking: Fear's Best Friend

Overthinking is like fear's partner-in-crime. You start analyzing every little detail, every possibility, and before you know it, you've convinced yourself that taking action is too risky.

Hmm, let's be honest—how many times have you talked yourself out of doing something because you thought about it too much? That's analysis paralysis. The more you think, the scarier things seem. Dam it, the mind is powerful, isn't it?

The 5-Second Rule

There's a simple trick to beat fear—act before your brain has time to talk you out of it. Mel Robbins calls it the 5-second rule:

1. You count down: 5, 4, 3, 2, 1.

2. You take action before fear kicks in.

That's it. Sounds too simple? Try it.

Next time fear tries to stop you, count down and move. No thinking. No analyzing. Just action.

The Power of Small Wins

Victory doesn't always mean huge achievements. Even small wins count. Every little step you take in spite of fear builds confidence.

Scared to talk to someone new? Say hello anyway.

Nervous about starting a project? Just write the first sentence.

Afraid of failure? Take a tiny risk.

Each small win weakens fear's hold on you. Oh shit, imagine where you'd be if you collected 1000 small wins instead of waiting for one big victory.

Fear and the Comfort Zone

Your comfort zone is fear's playground. As long as you stay inside it, fear wins. But the moment you step out, fear gets weaker.

Think about it—how many things that scared you in the past are now easy? That's because you faced them. Hahaha, remember when riding a bicycle seemed impossible? And now? It's nothing.

Fear fades when you expose yourself to it repeatedly. The more you do something, the less scary it becomes.

Victory is a Habit

Here's the real secret—winning over fear is a habit. The more you do it, the easier it gets.

Fear of public speaking? Start with small conversations.

Fear of failing in business? Start with a small project.

Fear of being judged? Put yourself out there anyway.

It won't happen overnight, but with practice, victory becomes your default mode.

Final Thoughts

Fear will never leave. But neither will victory. The choice is always in your hands. You can let fear control you, or you can take action despite it.

Hmm, let me ask you—what's one thing fear is stopping you from doing right now? Whatever it is, go do it. Count down: 5, 4, 3, 2, 1... and move.

Because fear may always exist, but dam it, so does victory. And it's waiting for you.

Wow, this was a long one, huh? But hey, if you've made it this far, that means you're ready to fight your fears. And that's already a victory. Hahaha, let's go win some more!

Why Be Afraid of Failure? Win or Learn

"Oh shit, I messed up!" Sounds familiar? Yeah, we've all been there. That moment when everything you planned just crumbles right in front of your eyes, and you feel like the biggest loser on the planet. But guess what? That's not failure. That's just a lesson in disguise.

Failure is like that strict teacher we all hated in school but later realized was actually shaping us into something better. So, why the hell do we fear it so much? Hmm... good question, right? Let's dive into this and figure out why failure isn't the villain but the damn superhero of your story.

---

1. The Stupid Stigma Around Failure

Society has made failure look like the ultimate curse. You fail, and suddenly everyone starts treating you like a lost cause. "Oh, poor guy, he failed." Hahaha, what nonsense! The truth is, every successful person has failed more times than they can count. But they didn't stop; they learned, adapted, and kept going.

Take Thomas Edison. The dude failed 1,000 times before making the light bulb. Can you imagine failing that much? Dam it, most of us quit after three tries! But Edison didn't. Why? Because he knew failure was just another step toward success.

---

2. Win or Learn: The Only Two Outcomes

Here's a mindset shift that will blow your mind—there are no failures, only two possibilities: Win or Learn. If you succeed, awesome! If you don't, well, you just got a valuable lesson. And guess what? That lesson makes you smarter, stronger, and more prepared for the next challenge.

Wow, imagine if we started seeing every setback as an opportunity to learn instead of an excuse to quit. Life would be so much easier, right?

---

3. The Pain of Regret vs. The Pain of Trying

Let's be real. Failure hurts. It stings like hell. But you know what's worse? Regret. Oh shit, that feeling of "What if I had tried?" is way more painful than any failure. At least if you try and fail, you'll have a lesson. If you don't try at all, you're left with nothing but regrets.

Hahaha, imagine sitting in a rocking chair at 80 years old, thinking, "I should have taken that risk." No way! Fail now, learn now, and move forward. Life is too short to play safe all the time.

---

4. Reframing Failure: It's Just Data!

Think of failure like a scientist does. Every failed experiment gives them data to make the next attempt better. That's exactly how you should see your failures.

Failed at a business? Good, now you know what not to do. Failed in a relationship? Great, now you understand what went wrong and how to improve.

Failure is just feedback. Nothing more, nothing less.

---

5. Fear is a Liar

Fear makes failure look 10 times scarier than it actually is. It whispers things like, "You're not good enough," "People will laugh at you," or "You'll never recover from this." But let's be honest—how many times have your worst fears actually come true? Hmm... exactly! Fear is mostly bullshit. It exaggerates problems and paralyzes you into inaction.

So, next time fear shows up, laugh at it. Hahaha, tell it, "Nice try, but I'm doing this anyway!"

---

6. The Fastest Path to Success? Fail More!

Want to succeed faster? Then fail faster! Look at all the greats—Michael Jordan, Steve Jobs, J.K. Rowling—they failed like crazy before they made it big. But they didn't stop. They kept taking swings until they hit the jackpot.

Most people fail once and give up. That's why they remain average. If you want to be extraordinary, you have to fail a lot. So, go out there and mess up. Again and again. Because every failure gets you one step closer to success.

---

7. Action Beats Overthinking Every Time

Overthinking is the cousin of fear. The more you think about failing, the scarier it looks. But action? Action kills fear instantly. The moment you take that first step, fear starts fading away.

So, instead of sitting and worrying, just start. Even if you fail, you'll be further ahead than if you had done nothing. Dam it, how simple is that?

---

8. Failure Builds Resilience (Your Superpower)

Every time you fail and get back up, you build resilience. And resilience is the superpower that separates winners from losers.

Successful people aren't the smartest or the luckiest; they're just the ones who refuse to stay down. Every setback makes them stronger. Every fall makes them tougher. And that's why they eventually win.

So, get punched by failure. Get knocked down. Then stand back up, smile, and say, "Is that all you got?" Hahaha!

---

9. Success is Just Failure... with Persistence

Success isn't about never failing. It's about failing enough times until you finally succeed. Think about it—every "overnight success" you see actually took years of failures, rejections, and setbacks.

The only difference between a winner and a loser? The winner didn't quit.

---

* **Conclusion**: Fail Proudly, Fail Loudly!

So, here's the deal: Stop fearing failure. Embrace it, learn from it, and keep going. Next time you fail, don't hide it. Own it. Be proud of it. Share your failure stories. Laugh about them. Hahaha, because failure isn't a badge of shame—it's a badge of honor.

Remember, you either win or learn—but you never truly fail. So, go out there, take risks, fall flat on your face, and then get back up stronger than before.

Because failure is not the opposite of success. It's the path to it.

Let's go! Wow, this is going to be legendary!

IV

LIFE IS NOT A WAITING ROOM

How many times have you felt like you're just waiting?

Waiting for the right time.

Waiting for the right opportunity.

Waiting for motivation.

But let me tell you something—life is not a waiting room.

You don't sit and wait for your turn. You get up and take it.

The Myth of the "Right Time"

"I'll do it when the time is right." "I'm just waiting for the perfect moment."

Yeah, we've all said this. And let's be real—it's a damn good excuse. It makes us feel smart, responsible, and patient. But here's the harsh truth: the right time is a myth.

1. The Illusion of Readiness

Look, nobody ever feels fully ready. Even the most successful people started when they felt unprepared. You don't wake up one day magically knowing everything. The only way to feel ready is to start before you're ready. Crazy, right? But that's how it works.

Think about it:

Was anyone truly ready to be a parent? Nope. They just figured it out.

Were the biggest entrepreneurs ready when they launched? Nope. They learned on the way.

Did every athlete feel ready for their first big game? Definitely not.

So why the hell are you waiting?

2. "One Day" Never Comes

Let's be honest. "One day" is the biggest lie we tell ourselves. We keep pushing things to some mythical future where conditions will be perfect.

Guess what?

There's never going to be a perfect day.

There's never going to be zero risks.

There's never going to be a moment when you have all the knowledge, confidence, and luck lined up like magic.

You either start now, or you spend your life watching others who did. Your choice.

3. Fear Masquerading as Logic

A lot of times, waiting for the "right time" is just fear in disguise. We convince ourselves that we're being logical, strategic, and smart. But deep down, we're just scared of failing, looking stupid, or struggling.

And let's get one thing straight: struggle is part of success.

You're going to mess up.

You're going to face problems.

You're going to have doubts.

But that's not a reason to stop. That's a sign you're actually moving forward.

4. How to Destroy the Waiting Mindset

So, how do you break free from the "right time" myth? Simple:

1. Set a deadline. Not "someday," but an actual date. Make it non-negotiable.

2. Start small. You don't have to do everything at once, just take the first damn step.

3. Embrace discomfort. If you feel scared, it means you're on the right track.

4. Stop overthinking. Action beats overanalysis. Every. Single. Time.

The best time to start was yesterday. The next best time? Right now.

Opportunities Don't Knock, You Have to Create Them

We love this idea that one day, opportunity will just show up. Like some magical door will open, someone will hand us the golden ticket, and boom—success.

Sorry to break it to you, but that's pure fantasy.

1. Opportunities Are Built, Not Found

Waiting for opportunity is like waiting for a winning lottery ticket—a waste of time. The people who seem "lucky" are actually the ones who created their own chances.

They networked while others sat at home.

They took risks while others played safe.

They practiced relentlessly while others just thought about improving.

Nobody's handing out success. You have to grab it.

2. Why Most People Miss Opportunities

Here's the brutal truth: opportunities don't always look like opportunities. Sometimes, they look like extra work. They look like risks. They look like stepping outside your comfort zone.

That internship you're ignoring? Could lead to your dream job.

That random event you don't feel like attending? Could introduce you to someone life-changing.

That uncomfortable skill you refuse to learn? Could be the difference between success and mediocrity.

The reason people miss opportunities is because they expect them to be obvious. But they never are.

3. Excuses Kill Opportunities

Ever heard these before?

"I don't have the right connections."

"I don't have enough experience."

"I'll wait until I have more confidence."

Blah, blah, blah. Excuses are just another way of saying, "I'm too scared to try."

Confidence comes from doing, not waiting. Connections come from putting yourself out there. Experience comes from starting. If you don't take action, you're just ensuring that nothing changes.

4. How to Create Your Own Opportunities

So, how do you stop waiting and start creating?

1. Say YES more often. Even when you feel unprepared.

2. Be visible. Nobody can offer you an opportunity if they don't know you exist.

3. Put in the work. Show up, even when nobody's watching.

4. Take risks. The safest path is usually the slowest one.

5. Be obsessed with learning. The more you know, the more doors you can open.

If you want an amazing life, stop waiting for someone to give it to you. Go make it happen.

Time Doesn't Stop for Anyone

Hmm, have you ever just sat there, staring at the clock, watching the seconds tick tick tick away? Damn it, time doesn't wait, does it? Oh shit, another minute just passed. Whether we move or stay still, time keeps running. It's like an unstoppable train, and if we don't jump on board, we're left standing at the station, wondering where everyone went.

The Illusion of Infinite Time

Wow, we often feel like we have a lot of time. "I'll start tomorrow," "Next Monday sounds like a better day to begin," "Maybe when I feel ready." But here's the hard truth—there is no perfect time. Time won't pause until you feel prepared. It won't wait for you to be in the mood. The days you waste today are the ones you'll regret tomorrow.

Hahaha, life is funny that way. We act like we have unlimited time, but the truth is, none of us know how much we have left. The biggest mistake? Thinking we have "plenty of time" when, in reality, we don't even know if we have tomorrow.

The Cost of Waiting

Let's be honest. How many times have you delayed something just because you didn't feel like doing it? Maybe it was a personal goal, a dream project, or just a simple task like exercising or learning a new skill. Every time we postpone, we unknowingly pay a price. And what's that price? Lost opportunities, regret, and a pile of unfinished dreams.

Think about this—opportunities don't wait. You miss one, and someone else grabs it. While you're waiting for the right moment, someone else is taking action. And guess what? They're getting ahead. Oh shit, that realization hits hard, doesn't it?

Action Over Excuses

So, what's stopping you? Fear? Doubt? The idea that you're not ready? News flash—no one is ever 100% ready. The ones who succeed are the ones who take action despite the uncertainty.

Hmm, think of it this way—when you're learning to swim, do you wait until you're completely confident before jumping into the water? No! You jump in, struggle a bit, and then learn. Life works the same way. You don't wait to be fully prepared. You take the plunge, figure things out, and keep going.

The Power of Small Steps

Oh shit, what if you fail? Well, here's another truth bomb—failure is part of the process. Every setback teaches something. Instead of fearing failure, what if you start seeing it as a stepping stone? You don't have to take massive leaps. Just small steps. One step today, another tomorrow, and before you know it, you're far ahead of where you started.

Hahaha, imagine if a baby waited until it was "completely ready" before taking its first step. Ridiculous, right? They fall, get up, try again. That's how progress works.

The Regret of Lost Time

Fast forward ten years. Imagine looking back at today. What will you see? A version of you who took action, made mistakes, learned, and moved forward? Or a version of you who kept waiting, hesitating, making excuses?

Damn it, that's a scary thought. The worst kind of pain isn't failure—it's regret. The regret of knowing you could have done something but didn't. That's why the best time to start is always now.

Final Thoughts

Hmm, so what's the takeaway here? Simple—time waits for no one. Either you take charge and use it wisely, or you let it slip through your fingers while making excuses. The choice is yours.

Wow, imagine where you could be a year from now if you just start today. That's the magic of time—it keeps moving, but when you move with it, amazing things happen.

So, what's it going to be? Are you hopping on this train, or are you going to let it leave without you? Dam it, make the right choice!

Have you ever looked back and thought, "Damn it, I should've done that instead of wasting time"? We all have. That regret, that sinking feeling—it's brutal. Time is like sand slipping through our fingers, and the worst part? Once it's gone, it never comes back.

The Heavy Weight of Regret

Regret is one of those things that hit you when it's too late. You think you have all the time in the world, and then one day—boom—you realize how much of it you've wasted. Whether it's hours scrolling through your phone, procrastinating on a dream, or simply being stuck in a cycle of overthinking, regret always shows up like an uninvited guest.

1. The Illusion That "There's Always Tomorrow"

"I'll start tomorrow." "Next week, for sure." "Maybe after this one last episode." Sounds familiar? Hahaha, we all do this. We convince ourselves that time is infinite, but in reality, it's a ticking clock. Before you know it, days turn into months, months into years, and then—oh shit—you're looking back, wishing you had started earlier.

2. The Guilt That Eats You Alive

When you waste time, the guilt follows. It creeps in slowly and then hits you like a truck. "I could've been so much further ahead if I had just started earlier." That thought alone is enough to mess with your mind. And the worst part? No one else is to blame. It's all on you. Dam it, right?

Understanding Why We Waste Time

If regret sucks so much, why do we keep wasting time? Simple. Because:

Comfort zones are addictive – It feels safe, and change is scary.

We fear failure – If we never start, we can't fail. Twisted logic, but hey, it's real.

Distractions are everywhere – Social media, TV, endless entertainment—everything is designed to keep us hooked.

We underestimate time – We think we have plenty of it, but reality says otherwise.

The Cost of Wasting Time

Wasting time doesn't just make you feel bad; it has real consequences. Let's break it down:

1. Missed Opportunities

Every second wasted is an opportunity lost. That business idea? Someone else started it. That skill you wanted to learn? Someone else mastered it. Life doesn't wait, and opportunities don't knock forever.

2. Unfulfilled Potential

You were meant to do something big. We all are. But wasted time keeps you stuck in mediocrity. You could've been amazing at something by now, but instead, you're still "thinking about it." Wow, what a waste.

3. The Pain of "What If"

"What if I had started earlier?" "What if I hadn't wasted all that time?" "What if I had just taken that chance?" The "what ifs" will haunt you. And trust me, they're worse than failure.

The Solution? Take Control NOW

Alright, enough of the depressing stuff. The good news? It's never too late. Regret is only permanent if you don't act. So let's fix it.

1. Accept That Time is Precious

No more excuses. No more "I'll do it later." Understand that time is the most valuable thing you have, and you can't afford to waste it.

2. Identify Your Time Wasters

Be honest with yourself. What's stealing your time? Social media? Procrastination? Netflix marathons? Cut down the junk.

3. Make a Plan and Execute

Stop overthinking. Just do it. Want to write a book? Start with one page. Want to get fit? Do 10 push-ups right now. Momentum beats motivation.

4. Set Deadlines for Yourself

Deadlines create urgency. If you don't set a deadline, you'll keep pushing things off. Give yourself a time limit and stick to it.

5. Surround Yourself With Action-Takers

Your environment matters. Hang out with people who push you forward, not those who drag you down.

6. Forgive Yourself and Move Forward

Yes, you've wasted time. But dwelling on it will only waste more. Forgive yourself, learn from it, and move forward with a fire inside you.

The Bottom Line

Time wasted is life wasted. Regret is painful, but inaction is worse. The only way to avoid future regret is to take action now. Start small, stay consistent, and make every second count.

So, are you going to keep wasting time, or are you going to do something about it?

Your choice.

Stop Planning, Start Living

Hah! How many times have you sat down with a notebook, a pen, and a whole strategy to change your life? You make a perfect plan—every step detailed, every problem anticipated, and every goal nicely broken into tiny little tasks. Feels good, right?

But then... what happens? You don't execute.

You sit there, rethinking, tweaking the plan, waiting for the right time, and BOOM—weeks, months, maybe even years pass, and you're still at the same place. Dam it!

1. Planning is a Trap

Planning makes us feel productive, but it's often just an illusion. You write things down, research endlessly, watch motivational videos, and convince yourself that you're working towards your goals. But are you really?

Nope. You're stuck in the planning loop—a never-ending cycle where you keep adjusting plans instead of actually doing something. It's comfortable, it's safe, and it gives a false sense of progress.

But life? Life is happening right now. And you? You're just sitting there, planning how to live it instead of actually living.

2. The "Right Time" is a Myth

Oh shit! This is where most people mess up. They think they'll start when the timing is perfect.

"I'll start my business when I have more money." "I'll travel when I have more free time." "I'll get fit when work gets less hectic."

Hahaha, guess what? That "right time" never comes. Something new will always come up—a new excuse, a new responsibility, a new distraction.

Waiting for the right time is just an elegant way of procrastinating.

3. Execution Beats Perfection

Let's get real—when was the last time you achieved something big just by planning? Exactly. Success happens when you take action, even if it's messy.

Your first step won't be perfect. You might stumble, you might fail, but at least you'll be moving forward. And moving forward is the only way to get anywhere in life.

Start before you feel ready. Start when it's inconvenient. Start when it's scary. But just start.

4. Fear of Failure is Useless

Hmm... let's be honest. What's the worst that could happen if you take action? Maybe you fail. Maybe people laugh at you. So what?

At least you'll have a story to tell. At least you'll know you tried.

Failure teaches more than endless planning ever will. It shows you what works, what doesn't, and how to improve. Every successful person you admire? They failed more times than you can imagine. The difference? They kept going.

5. Life is Happening Now

Close your eyes and imagine this: You're 80 years old, sitting in a chair, looking back at your life. Will you be proud of all the plans you made but never acted on?

Hell no!

You'll regret the things you didn't do, the risks you didn't take, the adventures you postponed.

Newsflash: Life doesn't wait for you. It moves on, with or without you. If you keep planning instead of living, you'll wake up one day and realize you missed it all.

6. Action Creates Confidence

The biggest reason people keep planning is fear. Fear of failure, fear of rejection, fear of judgment. But here's the thing—confidence doesn't come from planning. It comes from action.

Want to be more confident? Do things. Try. Fail. Get up and try again.

Every time you take action, you prove to yourself that you're capable. And the more you prove it, the less fear controls you.

7. The "Start Small" Hack

Okay, so you're convinced. You want to stop planning and start living. But how?

Simple: Take one tiny step today. Not tomorrow. Not next week. Today.

Want to get fit? Do 10 push-ups right now.

Want to start a business? Launch a simple website in an hour.

Want to travel? Book a ticket before fear kicks in.

No more overthinking. No more waiting. Just do it.

8. Stop Planning, Start Living

Hmm... let's wrap this up.

Planning is useful, but only to an extent. If you're using it as an excuse to delay action, it's time to wake up. Life isn't waiting for you to make the perfect plan. It's moving forward.

So stop overthinking. Stop waiting. Stop planning every damn detail.

Just live. Now.
Because honestly? That's the only way to truly win.
Now go. Take action. Live your damn life.
Your Comfort Zone is a Trap

Introduction: The Silent Prison

Hmm... ever felt like you're stuck in the same routine, doing the same things, day after day? It feels safe, predictable, and comfortable. But what if I told you that this so-called "comfort zone" is actually a trap? A trap so well-disguised that most people don't even realize they are caught in it? Oh shit, that sounds scary, right? Well, buckle up, because by the end of this, you'll see just how dangerous staying in your comfort zone really is.

What is the Comfort Zone?

Let's break it down. The comfort zone is that mental space where everything feels easy and familiar. You avoid risks, challenges, and uncertainty. It's like living in a cozy little bubble where nothing unexpected happens. Feels good, huh? But here's the kicker—nothing ever grows in the comfort zone!

It's like planting a seed in a pot but never watering it, never exposing it to the sun, never giving it room to grow. Over time, it just withers away. And that's exactly what happens to your potential when you refuse to step out of your comfort zone.

The Illusion of Safety

You might think, "Hey, staying in my comfort zone means I won't fail, I won't get hurt, I won't have to deal with stress." Wow, sounds like a good deal, right? Wrong!

Life doesn't stop just because you do. The world keeps moving, evolving, and growing. And if you stay in the same place, you're not staying safe—you're actually falling behind. Dam it, that realization hits hard!

The comfort zone tricks you into believing you're secure when, in reality, it's making you weaker. You stop developing new skills, your confidence fades, and before you know it, opportunities pass you by while you're too scared to grab them.

Why People Stay Stuck

So, why do we fall into this trap?

1. Fear of Failure: Nobody likes to fail, and stepping out of your comfort zone comes with the risk of messing up. But guess what? Failure is just a lesson in disguise.

2. Fear of Judgment: What if people laugh at me? What if they think I'm stupid? Hahaha, let them think whatever they want! Their opinions won't pay your bills or shape your future.

3. Fear of the Unknown: We like predictability. Taking a new path means facing uncertainty, and that freaks people out. But news flash—everything great lies on the other side of uncertainty.

Signs You're Stuck in the Comfort Zone

Think you're safe? Let's check. If you relate to any of these, congratulations—you're trapped:

You avoid trying new things because they make you anxious.

You stick to the same routine every day.

You talk about dreams but never act on them.

You let fear decide your actions.

You feel restless, like something is missing, but don't know what.

Oh shit! If you just nodded to most of these, it's time for a wake-up call.

How the Comfort Zone Kills Growth

Staying in your comfort zone stops you from:

Learning new skills

Meeting new people

Discovering new opportunities

Building confidence

Achieving your full potential

Life is about progress, and progress only happens when you push yourself. Think of a gym—if you keep lifting the same weight forever, you'll never get stronger. Same goes for life. No challenges = No growth. Simple!

Breaking Free: How to Escape the Comfort Zone

Alright, enough talking about the problem. Let's fix it. Here's how you can break free:

1. Do One Thing That Scares You Daily: Hmm... nervous about public speaking? Try talking in front of a mirror first. Then, speak in front of a friend. Baby steps, but keep moving.

2. Say YES More Often: When an opportunity comes, instead of saying, "Nah, I'm not ready," say, "Hell yes, let's do it!" You'll figure things out along the way.

3. Embrace Failure: Every mistake is just a lesson. The faster you fail, the faster you learn. It's like falling while learning to ride a bike—you get up and try again.

4. Change Your Routine: Take a different route to work. Try a new hobby. Eat something you've never had before. The small things matter.

5. Surround Yourself with Risk-Takers: If you hang out with people who challenge themselves, you'll be inspired to do the same. Energy is contagious!

6. Visualize Your Future: Where do you see yourself in five years if you keep living like this? If that thought makes you cringe, then you KNOW it's time to change.

The Magic That Happens Outside the Comfort Zone

When you finally step out, amazing things start happening:

You build insane confidence.

You develop new skills that make you stand out.

You become more fearless.

You realize you're capable of more than you ever imagined.

And the best part? The more you push yourself, the bigger your comfort zone gets. What used to scare you becomes normal, and you keep growing.

Final Thoughts: *The Choice is Yours*

At the end of the day, no one is going to force you out of your comfort zone. It's YOUR job to take that first step. Will it be scary? Yes. Will it be uncomfortable? Hell yes. But will it be worth it? 100% YES.

So, what's it gonna be? Stay in the safety of the comfort zone and watch life pass you by, or take control and start living?

The choice is yours. Choose wisely!

The One Day Lie

"One day, I will start exercising." "One day, I will quit this job and follow my passion." "One day, I will travel the world." "One day, I will finally take care of myself."

Sounds familiar? Hmm... we have all been there. The dream of "one day" is so comforting, so safe, and yet, so deceiving. It makes us believe that time is infinite, that opportunities will always wait for us, and that someday, magically, everything will fall into place. But, oh shit, reality is harsh. "One day" is the biggest lie we tell ourselves.

The Illusion of "One Day"

Why do we love saying "one day"? Simple. It makes us feel good. It tricks us into believing we are in control of our future while allowing us to avoid taking action in the present. Hahaha, what a joke! It's like standing in front of a locked door with a key in hand but telling yourself, "One day, I will open it," while complaining about being stuck outside.

The problem is, "one day" is a moving target. Today, it feels close. Tomorrow, it moves further away. And before you know it, years have passed, and that "one day" never came.

Why "One Day" Never Comes

1. Life Gets in the Way

Oh wow, who would have thought? Life is unpredictable. Responsibilities pile up, unexpected challenges arise, and before you know it, you're too busy to focus on what you really wanted to do.

2. Fear Disguised as Excuses

"I'm not ready yet." "I need more time." "I'll do it when things settle down." These aren't reasons; they are excuses. Fear of failure, fear of discomfort, fear of change—these fears whisper in your ear, convincing you that postponing is a wise choice. Dam it! It's not!

3. Perfectionism

You want the perfect moment, the perfect plan, and the perfect conditions. But guess what? Perfection is a myth. No situation will ever be 100% perfect. The best time to start is always now.

The Cost of Believing in "One Day"

Every time you postpone something to "one day," you are paying a hidden cost—regret.

Lost Opportunities: The job you never applied for, the skills you never learned, the business you never started—all of them could have changed your life.

Wasted Time: You think you have plenty of time, but time is ruthless. It moves forward whether you act or not.

Stagnation: While you wait for "one day," someone else is out there taking action, improving, growing, and moving ahead.

How to Break Free from the "One Day" Trap

1. Turn "One Day" into "Day One"

Instead of saying, "One day, I will...," say, "Today, I start..." No matter how small, take a step. Just one.

2. Set a Deadline

A dream without a deadline is just a wish. Decide when you will do it and stick to it.

3. Start Before You Feel Ready

If you wait to feel ready, you'll wait forever. Just start, and you'll figure things out along the way.

4. Kill the Perfectionist in You

Done is better than perfect. A messy start is still a start. Hahaha, even a bad first step is better than no step.

5. Remind Yourself: "Time is Non-Refundable"

Every day that passes is a day you'll never get back. Let that sink in.

Final Thoughts

"One day" is comforting but dangerous. It keeps you in a loop of inaction. It robs you of opportunities and growth. If you really want to do something, start today. Not tomorrow, not next week, not "one day." Right now.

Because the truth is, "one day" will never come. But today? Today is real, and today is yours to take action.

"So, what are you waiting for?"

V

THINKER THINK, DOERS CHANGE THE GAME

Have you ever met someone who always talks about big plans but never does anything?

They say, "One day, I'll start my own business."

They say, "One day, I'll get in shape."

They say, "One day, I'll change my life."

But that "one day" never comes. Because thinkers only think. It's the doers who change the game.

Ideas Are Worthless Without Action

Alright, let's get straight to the point—ideas mean nothing without action. Yeah, you heard that right. You can sit in your room, dream up the next billion-dollar startup, the next best-selling novel, or the ultimate fitness routine, but guess what? If you don't take action, it's as good as daydreaming.

The Harsh Reality of Ideas

Think about it. How many times have you come up with a genius idea, only to see someone else actually do it and make it big? Feels like a punch in the gut, right? That's because ideas are cheap. Execution is what gives them value.

Every single person has ideas. Some are brilliant, some are crazy, and some are downright ridiculous. But ideas alone don't change the world. It's the action behind them that does.

The "Someone Stole My Idea" Myth

Ever had an idea and then saw someone else bring it to life? And then you're sitting there like, "Damn, they stole my idea!" No, they didn't. They just acted on it while you were waiting for the perfect time, the right mood, or whatever excuse you gave yourself.

Ideas don't wait for you. Someone, somewhere, is thinking the same thing as you right now. The only difference is, one of you is going to act, and the other is going to wish they had.

Action is the Game Changer

An average idea with great execution beats a brilliant idea with no execution—every single time. Look at successful entrepreneurs, writers, athletes—they didn't sit around waiting for inspiration to strike. They took their ideas and ran with them. They failed, learned, and kept going.

Here's the truth: most people don't lack ideas. They lack execution. And execution is what separates dreamers from doers.

Perfection is a Trap

One of the biggest reasons people don't act on their ideas? Perfectionism. "I need to refine my idea first." "I need to plan everything out." "I need to wait until I'm 100%

ready."

Spoiler alert: You will never be 100% ready.

Waiting for the perfect moment is just an excuse. The first version of anything you do will probably suck, and that's okay. Start anyway. Adjust as you go. Perfectionism kills more dreams than failure ever will.

Small Actions Lead to Big Results

You don't have to take a giant leap. Start small. Write that first page. Make that first call. Take that first step. The momentum will build from there.

Successful people don't wait for motivation; they create it through action. The more you do, the more you learn, and the better you get.

Failure is Just Feedback

Most people don't act because they're afraid of failing. But here's the thing—failure is not the opposite of success. It's part of it. Every failure teaches you something that makes you better. The only real failure is not trying at all.

Conclusion

At the end of the day, ideas are nothing but thoughts until you act on them. Execution is what turns an idea into reality. So stop overthinking. Stop waiting. Stop making excuses.

Take action now. Because if you don't, someone else will.

How Doers Learn Faster?

Alright, let's get real. You've probably heard this a million times: "Experience is the best teacher." But why? Why do people who actually do things learn faster than those who just sit around thinking about doing them? Well, buckle up, because we're diving deep into this.

---

1. Learning by Doing vs. Learning by Thinking

Thinking about doing something and actually doing it are two completely different worlds. You can read every book about swimming, watch hundreds of tutorials, and even listen to experts talk about it. But the moment you step into deep water, all that theoretical knowledge won't help unless you've actually practiced.

Thinking is passive – it keeps you in the "what if" loop.

Doing is active – it forces you to deal with real challenges.

Action builds muscle memory – your brain and body adapt quicker when you practice.

A doer fails, adjusts, and improves. A thinker? They're still planning their first step.

---

2. Real-World Feedback Speeds Up Growth

When you take action, you get instant feedback. Let's say you want to start a business. Reading business books might give you insights, but actually launching a small project teaches you way more. You learn about marketing, customer behavior, handling money, and dealing with unexpected problems.

Feedback = Growth – Each mistake teaches you something new.

Adaptation = Speed – The more you adjust, the faster you learn.

Experience = Confidence – Action removes the fear of the unknown.

Thinkers overanalyze. Doers take action, face reality, and adjust accordingly.

---

3. Failure Becomes a Teacher, Not an Enemy

The biggest advantage of doers? They fail fast. But here's the twist – failing isn't bad. It's a shortcut to learning. When you take action, you see what works and what doesn't, and that speeds up your learning curve.

Fear of failure slows down thinkers.

Doers use failure as a learning tool.

Each failure teaches something new and sharpens skills.

Thomas Edison didn't "fail" 10,000 times while inventing the lightbulb. He discovered 10,000 ways that didn't work.

---

4. Action Builds Stronger Neural Pathways

Your brain loves patterns. The more you repeat something, the stronger the neural connections become. It's like carving a path in the jungle – the more you walk through it, the clearer and easier it becomes.

Thinking about running doesn't build endurance. Running does.

Thinking about writing doesn't make you a writer. Writing does.

Thinking about learning a skill doesn't make you an expert. Practicing does.

By taking action, you train your brain to adapt faster. That's why doers learn quickly.

---

5. The Power of Trial and Error

Let's talk about something called the Fail-Fix Formula –

- Try something.
- Fail or succeed.
- Analyze what went wrong or right.
- Make adjustments.
- Try again, but smarter.

Thinkers try to get everything perfect before starting. Doers start, fail, and get better with each attempt. This real-world experience compounds over time, making them experts faster.

---

6. The Confidence-Action Loop
Confidence doesn't come from thinking about doing something. It comes from actually doing it.
Action builds confidence.
Confidence leads to more action.
More action leads to mastery.
That's why people who take action learn at an insane speed – they're constantly in motion, adjusting and improving with each step.

---

7. The Myth of "Being Ready"
Most people wait for the perfect time, the perfect plan, the perfect opportunity. But the truth? You're never fully ready.
Doers understand this and start anyway.
They learn as they go, adapting on the fly.
This rapid execution cycle helps them master skills faster than those waiting for 'the right moment.'
Waiting is a trap. Action is the real teacher.

---

8. Learning Happens in the Real World, Not in Books Alone
Books and courses are great, but they're just a starting point. The real magic happens when you apply what you learn.
You don't become a great speaker by reading about public speaking. You become one by speaking.

You don't become a great coder by watching tutorials. You become one by coding.

You don't become a great entrepreneur by studying business. You become one by running a business.

Knowledge without application is just potential. Action turns it into real skill.

---

9. How to Become a Doer and Learn Faster

Alright, so how do you actually shift from a thinker to a doer? Here's a simple roadmap:

- Set a small goal: Don't overcomplicate things. Pick something small and achievable.
- Take immediate action: Even if it's tiny, start today.
- Embrace imperfection: Done is better than perfect.
- Get feedback: See what works and what doesn't.
- Adjust and improve: Learn from mistakes and keep going.
- Repeat the cycle: Action → Feedback → Adjustment → Growth.

Before you know it, you'll be learning at a speed that'll leave thinkers in the dust.

Conclusion: *Why Doers Will Always Outlearn Thinkers*

At the end of the day, knowledge is useless unless applied. Doers understand this. They don't get stuck in the trap of overthinking. They take action, fail fast, learn faster, and improve quicker than anyone waiting for the perfect plan.

So, what's the takeaway?

Stop overthinking. Start doing.

Embrace failure as a learning tool.

Use real-world experience to speed up your growth.

You don't have to be perfect. You just have to start. Because the fastest learners? They're the ones in the game, not on the sidelines.

Now go out there and make something happen.

Opportunities Favor the Action Takers

Introduction: The Illusion of Luck Ever looked at successful people and thought, "Damn, they got lucky!"? Maybe they did. But what if I told you that their "luck" had less to do with fate and more to do with action? Yeah, that's right! Opportunities don't just drop into people's laps while they binge-watch Netflix. They show up when you step up.

So, let's get this straight: If you're sitting around waiting for the universe to hand you golden opportunities, you're playing yourself. Opportunities favor the action takers. The ones who move, try, fail, learn, and repeat. If you're ready to stop waiting and start creating your own path, let's dive in!

---

1. The Myth of the Perfect Opportunity

Raise your hand if you've ever said: "I'm waiting for the right time." Yeah? Well, here's a secret: The right time doesn't exist.

There will always be something in the way—lack of experience, fear, doubt, whatever. If you're waiting for all lights to turn green before you go, you'll never leave the house.

The best opportunities often look messy at first. They don't come with flashing neon signs saying, "THIS IS YOUR CHANCE!" They come disguised as challenges, risks, or even failures.

The people who win? They take a chance even when it doesn't feel like the perfect moment.

Example: Steve Jobs didn't wait for perfection. He built Apple in his garage. Was it the "right time"? Nope. But he made it the right time.

---

2. The "I'll Start Tomorrow" Trap

You ever told yourself, "I'll start next Monday"? Or "Next month, for sure"? Yeah, we've all been there. But let's be real—if you keep pushing things to "later," later never comes.

Procrastination is a silent killer of dreams. The longer you wait, the harder it gets.

Action builds momentum. The smallest step today is more powerful than the biggest plan for tomorrow.

Opportunities are perishable. They expire if you don't grab them.

Solution: Start now. Right now. Even if it's messy. Even if you don't know everything yet.

---

3. Taking Risks: The Price of Opportunity

Opportunities and risks are best friends. You can't have one without the other.

Every successful person has taken risks. Some paid off, some didn't. But they learned.

Fear of failure holds people back. But failure isn't the opposite of success—it's part of the journey.

If you avoid risks, you avoid growth. And if you avoid growth, you miss opportunities.

Example: Elon Musk bet everything on Tesla and SpaceX. He could've played it safe, but instead, he went all in. Now, look where he is.

---

4. Execution Over Ideas

Got an idea? Great! Now what? Because ideas alone are worthless without action.

People spend years "planning" but never execute. That's just fancy procrastination.

The real magic is in doing. Testing. Failing. Adjusting. Trying again.

Done is better than perfect. Perfectionism kills more dreams than failure ever will.

Truth: You don't need more ideas. You need more execution.

---

5. Hard Work > Talent

Sure, talent is cool. But hard work beats talent when talent doesn't work hard.

Plenty of talented people go nowhere because they don't put in the effort.

Meanwhile, average people who grind consistently get ahead.

Hard work creates luck. The more you work, the more "lucky breaks" you seem to get.

Example: Michael Jordan wasn't born the greatest basketball player. He worked harder than everyone else. Period.

---

6. Stop Waiting for Permission

You don't need permission to chase opportunities.

Too many people wait for someone to say, "Go for it!" Just start.

The world rewards those who take initiative.

No one is coming to save you. You have to be your own hero.

Truth: If you want something, take it. No one is stopping you but yourself.

---

7. The Power of Consistency

Success isn't about big wins. It's about showing up every damn day.

Small daily actions lead to massive results over time.

Consistency beats intensity. One crazy day of work doesn't matter if you quit the next.

The best opportunities come to those who prove they're serious.

Example: Writers don't become bestsellers overnight. They write every single day. Athletes don't win by training once. They train daily.

---

8. Surround Yourself with Action-Takers

Your environment matters. A lot.

If you're around lazy, excuse-making people, guess what? You'll become one too.

But if you surround yourself with action-takers, you'll level up fast.

The right circle pushes you to grab opportunities instead of making excuses.

Truth: Your network can be your shortcut—or your downfall. Choose wisely.

Conclusion: *Just Take the Damn Shot*

Look, opportunities don't wait. They don't care if you're scared, busy, or unsure. They reward those who take action.

Stop overthinking.

Stop waiting for the perfect moment.

Stop doubting yourself.

> "*Just start. Right now. Because the ones who move, who try, who push forward? They're the ones who*

win. Every. Single. Time."

VI

NO ONE CARES, SO STOP OVERTHINKING

Why We Overthink

Hmmm... so you turned on this? Damn it, bro! That means you overthink too, huh? Haha, don't worry, you're not alone. We all do it. Some more, some less, but everyone overthinks at some point. So let's talk about this thing—why do we overthink? And most importantly, HOW THE HELL DO WE STOP?

What is Overthinking?

Okay, so first, let's clear this up. Overthinking is like a broken replay button in your brain. Same thoughts, again and again, like an annoying song stuck in your head. Imagine you sent a risky text to someone, and now your brain is on fire. "What if they don't reply? What if they take it the wrong way? What if I made a typo?"

Boom! There goes your peace. You stare at your phone like it's some sort of magical object that will answer all your questions. You check 'Last Seen,' you stalk their Insta, you even start re-reading your own text 10 times. RELAX, bro. This is overthinking.

Why Do We Overthink?

1. We Care Too Much

Let's be honest. We want to be liked. We want to be right. We want things to go our way. And when something is uncertain, BOOM—our brain goes into detective mode. "What did I do wrong?" "What if this happens?" It's our mind trying to protect us, but honestly, it's doing the OPPOSITE.

2. Fear of Making Mistakes

Oh shit, this is a big one. Nobody likes screwing up. Imagine you have an exam tomorrow. Instead of studying, you're lying in bed, thinking, "What if I fail?" or "What if the questions are too hard?" Instead of finding a solution, your brain is running a horror movie marathon.

3. We Live in the Past

Sometimes, we sit and think about that one embarrassing moment from five years ago. "Why did I say that?" "Why did I act like that?" Newsflash, bro—the people who were there probably don't even remember it. But YOU do. And you keep replaying it like a Netflix series. WHY??

4. We Want a Perfect Future

A lot of overthinking is about the future. "Will I succeed?" "Will I get that job?" "What if I make the wrong decision?" We want to be 100% sure before making a move. But guess what? Life doesn't work like that! No one knows the future. Even Google doesn't.

How to Stop Overthinking?

1. Ask Yourself: Will This Matter in 5 Years?

Next time you overthink, ask yourself: "Will I even remember this in five years?" If not, STOP STRESSING. Seriously.

2. Distract Yourself

Overthinking loves silence. If you sit alone doing nothing, your brain will throw a thousand useless thoughts at you. So, do something. Go for a walk, listen to music, watch a movie, call a friend. Whatever keeps your brain busy.

3. Take Action

Thinking too much about a problem? Just do something about it. Overthinking never solved anything. Action does. If you're stuck in 'what ifs,' switch to 'What can I do NOW?'

4. Limit Your Thinking Time

This is a cool trick. If your brain wants to overthink, fine. But give it a time limit. Say, "I'll think about this for 10 minutes, and then I'll move on." Once time's up, let it go.

5. Accept That You Can't Control Everything

Bro, you are NOT a god. You can't control how people react, you can't predict the future, and you DEFINITELY can't change the past. Accept it. Focus on what you CAN do.

Final Thoughts

Look, overthinking is normal. But don't let it CONTROL you. The truth is—most of the things we overthink never even happen. It's just our brain messing with us. So next time your mind goes on an overthinking spree, just tell yourself: "STOP! This isn't helping."

Because at the end of the day, life is simple. Don't think too much. Just do it.

Hmmm... got it? Now go, live your life, and stop overthinking! Haha.

And if you still don't understand, you can stop

Let's go

Alright, let's get straight to it. No one is watching you.

Wait, wait... before you get all defensive, let me explain.

We live in a world where we THINK people care about what we do. We stress about how we look, how we talk, what we post on social media, and how others perceive us. But here's the bitter pill you need to swallow—NO ONE CARES.

Hmmm... I know, that stings a little. But honestly, it should be the most freeing thing ever.

The Illusion of Spotlight

Ever heard of the Spotlight Effect? It's a psychological thing. Basically, we believe that we are constantly being watched, judged, and analyzed by people around us. Oh shit, did I just stutter while speaking? Dammit, everyone must think I'm dumb. Oh wow, I wore the same shirt twice this week... people must think I'm broke.

Nah, bro. No one even noticed.

Everyone is too busy thinking about themselves to care about what YOU are doing. Just like you overthink your own actions, they are overthinking theirs. It's like a never-ending loop of people thinking about themselves and assuming others are thinking about them.

Social Media Made It Worse

Oh wow, let's post a perfect picture, add a deep caption, and wait for the likes to roll in. Hahaha, sounds familiar? We spend hours thinking about the perfect selfie, the perfect angle, the perfect words... and for what? For some random people to double-tap on their screen while they're mindlessly scrolling?

Dammit, we've been fooled.

You post something, and yeah, people might see it. Maybe they'll like it, maybe they won't. But do you really think they'll REMEMBER it a week later? Hell no. Because the next minute, they're onto the next post, the next trend, the next distraction.

Fear of Judgment is a Trap

How many times have you stopped yourself from doing something just because of the fear of what people will think? Hmmm... let's see:

Didn't wear that outfit because "people will judge."

Didn't start that YouTube channel because "what if no one likes it?"

Didn't ask that question in class because "what if they think I'm dumb?"

Wow. We're basically giving up on things just because of imaginary opinions that probably don't even exist.

And even if people DO judge you? So what? They'll forget about it in a day. You, on the other hand, will be stuck with regrets. Damn, that's a tough trade.

The Freedom in Accepting the Truth

Once you accept that no one is actually watching, life becomes easier.

You stop caring about dumb opinions.

You wear what you like.

You speak your mind.

You do what makes YOU happy, not what makes others impressed.

Hahaha, imagine how light that feels! When you don't have to carry the weight of unnecessary expectations on your shoulders, life becomes so much more fun.

Final Thoughts

Listen up. No one is watching you as much as you think they are.

Stop overanalyzing. Stop hesitating. Stop living for others.

Just go out there and do your thing.

Because the harsh truth is... no one is watching. And that's the best thing ever.

Real vs Imaginary Problems

Okay, let's get real for a second. We all have problems, right? Some are real, some are just in our heads. But the tricky part? Most of the time, we don't even know the difference!

Hmmm... think about it. How many times have you stressed over something that never actually happened? Like, you thought your best friend was ignoring you, but turns out they were just busy. Or you kept thinking you'd fail an exam, but you actually passed? That's an imaginary problem!

Now, let's talk about real problems. Like, if you don't study at all and then fail—yeah, that's a real problem. If your bank account is at zero and you need to pay rent—real problem! If you're stuck in a toxic relationship and it's draining your energy—real freakin' problem!

So, why do we stress more about imaginary problems? Simple. Our brain is an overthinker. It loves to create problems that don't exist. And we let it! Oh shit, that's dangerous.

How to Identify Real vs Imaginary Problems?

1. Ask yourself: Is it happening right now? If yes, real problem. If no, imaginary.

2. Can you take action on it? Real problems need action. Imaginary problems need you to chill.

3. Is it based on facts or assumptions? If you're just assuming something will go wrong, that's an imaginary problem, my friend.

What To Do About Imaginary Problems?

Laugh at them. Seriously, when you realize how silly they are, they lose power.

Focus on the present. If it's not happening now, why waste your energy?

Remind yourself: Not every thought is true. Just because your brain says something doesn't make it a fact.

What To Do About Real Problems?

Take action. Sitting and crying won't fix it.

Break it down. If the problem looks huge, divide it into smaller steps.

Accept what you can't control. Some things are just out of our hands. Let them go.

Hahaha, life becomes so much easier when you stop fighting imaginary problems and start focusing on real ones. So, next time your brain throws a problem at you, take a step back and ask, "Is this even real? Or is my brain just messing with me again?"

Damn it, we really do overthink too much!

The Cost of Wasted Time

Hmmm... So, you think time is just slipping away? Ever felt like you had a whole day, and suddenly it's gone? Poof! Just like that. And then you sit there, thinking, "Where did all my time go?" Well, welcome to the harsh reality, my friend. Time is that one currency you can never earn back. Once it's gone, it's gone. Damnnn, that hurts, right?

The Illusion of "Later"

"I'll do it later."

Ohhh, the biggest scam we sell ourselves daily. Tell me, how many times have you said this? And be honest! You had a plan, a goal, a task... and then BOOM, distractions took over. Maybe it was scrolling Instagram, watching that one more episode, or just lying in bed, thinking, "Meh, I'll do it tomorrow." But does tomorrow ever come? Nah, because when it does, you say "later" again. And before you know it—weeks, months, even years just vanish. Poof!

Time Is a Ruthless Judge

Here's the thing—time doesn't care about your excuses. It won't pause because you're not "feeling like it." It won't wait because you had a rough day. It just moves. And guess what? There's someone out there, right now, using their time wisely—hustling, learning, growing. And you? Still thinking, still waiting, still wasting. Ouch.

The Silent Regret

Oh shit, this one stings.

Think about this—five years from now, will you look back and be proud of how you used your time? Or will you slap yourself, thinking, "I should have started back then"? Nothing is worse than regret. That feeling of "I could have done so much more."

Hahaha, scary, right? But this is reality, bro. No sugar-coating.

Your Time is Your Responsibility

No one will come and save your time for you. No one will push you to do the right thing. It's YOU vs. YOU. Every damn day. So stop waiting for motivation. Just get up and start. Even if it's messy. Even if it's slow. Just start. Because every second counts, and wasted time... well, that's just a debt you can never repay.

So, what will you do next? Keep scrolling? Or finally take charge of your time?

The Reality Check

Let's be real for a second—99% of the things we overthink never even happen. Think about it. How many times have you worried about something, lost sleep over it, only to realize later that it wasn't a big deal? Overthinking makes tiny problems look massive, and imaginary fears feel real. But guess what? Most of these thoughts are just illusions, created by our own minds.

How to Break the Cycle?

Alright, so how do we escape this overthinking prison? Simple steps:

1. Awareness is the Key – The moment you catch yourself overthinking, pause. Ask yourself, "Is this thought even real?"

2. Take Action – Thinking endlessly won't change anything. If something is bothering you, do something about it instead of just thinking about it.

3. Distract Your Mind – Get up, take a walk, do some push-ups, or listen to music. Give your brain a break.

4. Talk it Out – Sometimes, sharing your thoughts with a friend helps you realize how silly your worries actually are.

5. Limit Your 'What Ifs' – Whenever you start a sentence with "What if...", remind yourself that it's just an assumption, not reality.

Final Thoughts

Overthinking is like sitting in a rocking chair—it gives you something to do but takes you nowhere. So, why waste time in your own mind's maze? Break the cycle, take charge, and live freely.

Life is too short to be stuck in endless thoughts. Get up and move forward!

The Role of Confidence

Hmmm... confidence! That magical thing we all want but sometimes struggle to have. You know that feeling when you walk into a room, and everyone just seems so sure of themselves? Like, damn, how do they do that? Well, the truth is, confidence isn't something you're just born with—it's built, step by step.

Confidence vs. Fake Confidence

Let's get one thing straight. Confidence is not about acting like you know everything. That's just arrogance. Real confidence is knowing that even if you don't have all the answers, you can figure things out. Fake confidence is loud, real confidence is quiet but unshakable.

Why Confidence Matters

Think about it. Ever noticed how confident people seem to get more opportunities? It's not because they're better, it's because they believe they can do it. Confidence helps you take risks, meet new people, and chase your dreams without overthinking every little detail. It's like a cheat code for life.

The Harsh Truth: No One Cares

Oh yeah, let's address this. Sometimes we hold back because we think people are watching and judging us. News flash: they're not. Everyone is too busy worrying about themselves. So stop doubting and start doing!

How to Build Confidence?

1. Take Small Wins – You don't become confident overnight. Start with small victories. Set tiny goals and achieve them. It adds up.

2. Face Your Fears – Confidence grows when you push past discomfort. Do the thing that scares you a little, and you'll realize it's not that bad.

3. Body Language – Stand straight, make eye contact, speak clearly. Your body fools your brain into feeling more confident.

4. Surround Yourself with Positivity – Confidence is contagious. Hang out with people who uplift you, not those who drain you.

5. Stop Seeking Approval – You don't need validation to be worthy. The more you trust yourself, the less you care about what others think.

Confidence is Like a Muscle

You don't wake up one day and suddenly become super confident. It's like going to the gym. The more you exercise it, the stronger it gets. Start now, and soon, you'll be the one walking into a room making others wonder, "Damn, how do they do that?"

So, what's stopping you from being confident today?

Stop Seeking Validation

Hey you! Yes, you.

Let's have a real talk today. Just you and me. No filters, no sugarcoating, just pure, raw truth. And today's truth is something you NEED to hear – **STOP SEEKING VALIDATION.**

Hmmm... feels a bit personal, doesn't it? Like I just exposed you? Relax, I'm not judging you. We all do it. Every single one of us. But here's the deal: seeking validation is like drinking salt water—no matter how much you get, you'll always be thirsty.

Why Do We Seek Validation?

Let's start with the basics—why the hell do we even care so much about what others think?

We grew up in a world where approval = success. Since childhood, we were told to get good grades, behave well, and impress others. Basically, "Be a good kid so people like you."

Social media has messed up our heads. One like? Meh. Ten likes? Cool. A hundred? Damn, I'm famous! And if nobody reacts? Oh shit, am I invisible?

We fear rejection. Let's be honest, getting ignored or judged HURTS. So we keep adjusting ourselves to fit in, to be liked, to be accepted.

But here's the thing—living for validation is like being a puppet, and guess who's holding the strings? EVERYONE BUT YOU.

The Harsh Truth

Now, I hate to break it to you, but nobody actually cares. Wait, wait, don't get mad! Hear me out.

People are too busy worrying about their own lives, their own problems, and their own insecurities to think about you 24/7. Yeah, maybe they'll judge you for a few minutes, maybe they'll laugh at you for a day, but then? They move on.

Meanwhile, you're still stuck, overthinking what they might be thinking about you. See the irony?

Signs You're Addicted to Validation

Let's do a quick self-check. If you relate to these, we got a problem:

You constantly check who viewed your story, who liked your post, and who didn't.

You change your decisions based on what others might think.

You feel anxious if you don't get compliments or approval.

You say yes to things you don't even like just to fit in.

Sound familiar? That's validation addiction. And it's killing your confidence, your happiness, and your freedom.

How to Stop Seeking Validation

Alright, time to break free. Let's fix this mess.

1. Realize That You Are Enough

Nobody's approval will ever make you truly happy. Read that again. The day you start believing that your worth is not tied to others' opinions, you'll feel unstoppable.

2. Post, Speak, Do... Without Overthinking

Next time you want to post something or express your opinion, JUST DO IT.

Not because people will like it. Not because you'll get praise. But because YOU WANT TO.

3. Ask Yourself: Do I Even Like This?

Are you doing things because YOU like them or because you want others to approve? Be brutally honest with yourself.

4. Reduce Social Media Time

Social media is the biggest validation trap. Try a detox for a day or two. It'll feel weird at first, but trust me, you'll feel lighter, freer.

5. Embrace Being Unliked

Not everyone will like you. And that's okay. In fact, if everyone likes you, you're probably fake as hell.

6. Find Internal Validation

Instead of waiting for someone to tell you, "You look good," stand in front of the mirror and say it yourself. Instead of waiting for someone to say, "You did great," recognize your own efforts.

Validation should come from WITHIN, not from likes, comments, or applause.

Final Thoughts

Listen, seeking validation is human nature. But depending on it is dangerous.

You weren't born to impress others. You were born to LIVE. To create. To express. To be YOU.

So the next time you catch yourself waiting for approval, remind yourself:

"I don't need their validation. I validate myself."

And that, my friend, is freedom.

The Worst Case Scenario Exercise

Hmmm... huh? Overthinking every possible way things could go wrong? Damn it, we've all been there! But let me ask you—have you ever really thought about the absolute worst case scenario? Like, REALLY thought about it? No sugarcoating, no escaping. Just facing it head-on.

You see, our brains are like overprotective parents. The moment we step out of our comfort zone, it screams, "Oh shit! What if everything goes wrong?" And suddenly, you're trapped in an endless loop of "what ifs." Hahaha, been there, done that, my friend.

But here's the real deal—the Worst Case Scenario Exercise. It's simple, and trust me, it's gonna hit different once you actually try it.

Step 1: Define The Fear

Alright, take a deep breath. Now think about that thing—the one that's haunting your mind. It could be a decision, a risk, a dream you're scared to chase. Whatever it is, write it down. Be brutally honest.

For example:

"I want to quit my job and start my own thing, but what if I fail?"

"I like someone, but what if they reject me?"

"I want to post my work online, but what if people hate it?"

Okay, now that we've pulled that fear out into the open, let's dissect it.

Step 2: The Absolute Worst-Case Scenario

Now, let's go wild. Imagine the most dramatic, catastrophic failure possible. No limits.

For example:

You quit your job, your business fails, you lose all your money, and end up broke.

You confess your feelings, get rejected, and feel like a fool.

You post your work, people make fun of it, and you never recover from the humiliation.

Hahaha, sounds terrifying, right? But hold on, we're not done.

Step 3: What Happens Then?

Now ask yourself: If the worst case happens, what will you do? Seriously, what's your next step?

You lose all your money? Cool. You get a part-time job, rebuild, and try again.

You get rejected? Alright, you move on and find someone who actually appreciates you.

People make fun of your work? Hmmm... So what? You improve, keep creating, and eventually, those same people shut up.

Oh wow. Look at that. You survive.

Step 4: The Best Case Scenario

Now that we've handled the worst, let's flip the coin. What's the best thing that could happen?

Your business actually works, and you build a life you love.

The person you like says yes, and it's the start of something amazing.

People love your work, and you build a community around it.

Hmmm... kinda exciting, right?

Step 5: Reality Check

Here's the final blow: How likely is the worst-case scenario, really?

Most of the time, it's not even close to happening. Our brain just loves to exaggerate. Think about it: Has your life ever completely fallen apart over one decision? Even when things went wrong, didn't you find a way out?

This exercise isn't about ignoring risks. It's about seeing them clearly and realizing they're not as scary as your brain makes them out to be.

Final Thoughts

Next time you're stuck in the overthinking loop, grab a paper, run through these steps, and OWN your fear. Because at the end of the day, the worst-case scenario is rarely as bad as we imagine.

And the best-case scenario? Well... that's waiting for you to take the first step.

So, what's stopping you?

"Your Move:"

1. Think of one thing you've been overthinking about.

2. Ask yourself—Will this matter in five years? If not, let it go.

3. Take action today, without worrying about people's opinions.

No one cares as much as you think they do. So, stop overthinking and start living.

VII

YOUR MINDSET IS YOUR SUPERPOWER

Fixed vs Growth Mindset

Hmmm... ever noticed how some people just keep improving while others stay stuck? Like, no matter what happens, some folks bounce back stronger, while others? Well, they just give up. The secret? It all comes down to mindset—***Fixed vs Growth.***

Oh, wait! Before we dive deep, let's be real for a sec. No fancy words, no complicated psychology—just straight-up truth. Ready? Let's go!

What the heck is a Fixed Mindset?

A fixed mindset is like believing that everything about you is set in stone. Your intelligence, your talents, your abilities—all fixed. If you suck at math, you'll always suck at math. If you're bad at public speaking, you'll always be bad at it. DAMN! Sounds depressing, right?

But wait—it gets worse. People with a fixed mindset avoid challenges because they're scared of failing. Oh shit! Failure? That's their biggest nightmare. So what do they do? They stick to what they already know, stay inside their comfort zone, and never try anything new. The result? ZERO growth.

You know that friend who always says, "I'm just not a creative person" or "I'm not good at sports"? Yeah... they're trapped in a fixed mindset without even realizing it. And the worst part? They actually believe it!

Now, what about the Growth Mindset?

Here's where things get exciting. A growth mindset is all about believing you can improve. Intelligence, skills, confidence—it's all learnable. You're not stuck; you're evolving.

People with a growth mindset embrace challenges. They're like, "Oh, I failed? Hahaha! Let's try again!" They actually see failure as a lesson, not a dead end. Imagine that! Instead of being scared of mistakes, they use them as stepping stones.

This mindset is what makes people unstoppable. You ever wonder how someone goes from broke to millionaire? Or from failing school to becoming a top entrepreneur? BOOM! Growth mindset. They learn, adapt, improve, and keep moving forward.

Fixed vs Growth: The HARSH Reality

Let's be brutally honest here. A fixed mindset is a TRAP. It makes you believe you can't improve, so you don't even try. And guess what? If you don't try, you stay stuck. And when you stay stuck, life just passes you by. Ouch.

Meanwhile, a growth mindset unlocks doors. It helps you become better, stronger, smarter—just by shifting the way you THINK.

Want proof? Look around! Successful people weren't born successful. They failed, learned, and grew. From Steve Jobs to Elon Musk to that kid who was failing math but kept practicing until he aced it—growth mindset ALL THE WAY.

How to Switch to a Growth Mindset?

Oh, now we're talking! If you're stuck in a fixed mindset, don't panic. Here's how you can shift gears:

1. Catch your thoughts. When you say, "I can't do this," STOP. Flip it: "I can't do this... YET."

2. Challenge yourself. Step out of that damn comfort zone! Try new things, even if you suck at first.

3. Learn from failure. Instead of crying over mistakes, ask, "What can I learn from this?"

4. Surround yourself with growth-minded people. Avoid those who say "It's impossible." Find those who say "Let's figure it out."

5. Celebrate progress, not perfection. You don't have to be great instantly. Small wins add up!

The Final Truth (No Sugarcoating!)

Listen, you have TWO choices:

1. Stay in a fixed mindset and let life pass you by.

2. Develop a growth mindset and take control of your future.

Simple, right? But here's the kicker: ONLY YOU CAN DECIDE. No one is going to do it for you. You either stay stuck OR start growing.

So, what's it gonna be? Fixed or growth? The choice is yours...

Hmmm...

Think about it.

How Your Mindset Shapes Your Reality

Hey, hey! Let's talk about something super important today—your mindset. Yeah, that thing inside your head that decides whether you'll conquer the world or just sit there scrolling through your phone, feeling stuck. You ever wonder why some people seem to have all the luck, while others are always struggling? Well, spoiler alert—it's not luck. It's their mindset.

The Invisible Force Controlling Your Life

Think about this—your thoughts are like a lens. If you've got a dirty lens (negative mindset), everything looks blurry, dark, and hopeless. But if your lens is clean and clear (positive, growth-oriented mindset), the world suddenly looks full of possibilities. Hmmm... interesting, right?

Oh, and before you think, "Nah, this is just some motivational crap," let me tell you—this is SCIENCE, my friend. Your mindset literally shapes your actions, your beliefs, and ultimately, your reality.

Fixed vs. Growth Mindset (A Quick Recap)

Okay, let's break it down. There are two kinds of people in this world:

1. Fixed Mindset Gang: They believe abilities, intelligence, and talents are set in stone. "I'm just not good at math." "I'll never be confident." Sound familiar? Dammit, this mindset is dangerous!

2. Growth Mindset Squad: They believe skills can be developed with effort, practice, and learning. They see challenges as opportunities. "I can get better at this." "I'll figure it out." Ohhh, now we're talking!

Your Mindset Decides How You React

Imagine two people lose their jobs. One goes, "Oh shit! My life is over." The other says, "Okay, this sucks, but maybe it's a chance to do something better." SAME SITUATION. Two totally different reactions. Why? Because their mindset is different.

See, life throws punches at everyone. But whether you get knocked out or stand back up depends on your mindset.

The Self-Fulfilling Prophecy (Oh, It's Real!)

Let's say you believe you're bad at public speaking. Because of this belief, you never practice, you avoid situations where you have to speak, and guess what? You suck at it. And then you say, "See? I told you I'm bad at it." Ummm, bro, YOU made it true!

But flip it—believe you can improve, take small steps, practice, and BOOM! One day, you're the person on stage, owning it. Your mindset literally creates your reality.

The "Everything is Figureoutable" Attitude

Successful people don't have all the answers. But they believe they can figure it out. That's the key! Instead of saying, "I don't know," start saying, "I don't know yet." That small change in words? Yeah, it rewires your brain.

Stop Playing the Victim

Harsh truth? No one is coming to save you. If you sit around waiting for things to get better on their own, you'll be waiting forever. Successful people take charge. They don't blame the economy, their parents, or their past. They focus on what they can control.

Your Reality is a Reflection of Your Mindset

If you see problems, you'll find more problems.

If you see opportunities, you'll find more opportunities.

If you believe the world is against you, guess what? It'll feel like it is.

If you believe the world is full of possibilities, suddenly, doors start opening.

Hahaha, sounds like magic, right? But it's not. It's just how the brain works.

How to Rewire Your Mindset (Yes, You Can!)

Alright, let's get practical. ***Here's how you can shift your mindset starting today:***

1. Catch Your Thoughts – Start noticing negative self-talk. Would you say those things to a friend? No? Then don't say them to yourself.

2. Reframe Challenges – Instead of "This is hard," say, "This is a chance to grow."

3. Surround Yourself with Growth-Minded People – Energy is contagious. Choose wisely.

4. Celebrate Small Wins – Progress, no matter how small, is still progress.

5. Keep Learning – Read, listen, grow. Your brain is a muscle—use it!

Final Thoughts

Look, your mindset isn't some tiny thing—it's EVERYTHING. It decides what kind of life you'll live. So, what's it gonna be? Are you gonna stay stuck in a fixed mindset, or are you gonna level up and shape your own damn reality?

The choice is yours. But remember—*your future self is watching.*

Now go out there and create the life you want!

The Power of a Solution-Oriented Mindset

Hmmm... ever felt stuck in a problem so bad that it feels like a dead end? Like, no way out? Damn, that feeling sucks, right? But wait, have you ever met those people who, no matter what happens, always seem to have an answer? Like, their world is also on fire, but they're just casually roasting marshmallows over it? That's the magic of a solution-oriented mindset.

Let's talk about this. Why? Because if you get this, life will stop feeling like a never-ending maze. You'll find your way out, every single time.

The Trap of Problem-Focused Thinking

Most people do this (and let's be real, we all do at some point). You face a problem, and then what happens?

Overthinking kicks in. "Why did this happen? Why me? This is so unfair."

You start playing the blame game. "It's because of them. If only they did this or that..."

You get stuck in negative loops. "I can't do anything about it. I'm helpless."

And guess what? Nothing changes. Nothing improves. You're just drowning in your own thoughts, and the problem still exists. Ouch.

The Shift: Solution-Oriented Thinking

A solution-oriented mindset flips the game. Instead of crying over problems, you instantly switch to finding ways to solve them. Imagine you spill coffee on your white shirt before an important meeting. A problem-focused person will freak out, complain, maybe even cancel the meeting. A solution-oriented person? They'll grab a jacket, borrow a new shirt, or simply own the coffee-stained look with confidence. Simple shift, massive difference.

How to Develop a Solution-Oriented Mindset

Okay, so how do you rewire your brain to stop panicking and start solving? Let's break it down.

1. Pause the Drama, Ask the Right Question

Instead of asking, "Why is this happening to me?", switch to "What can I do about this?" This small change forces your brain to think forward instead of being stuck in a loop.

2. Detach from the Emotion

Oh man, emotions are tricky. When you're frustrated, angry, or scared, you make terrible decisions. The key? Step back. Take a deep breath. Detach. Look at the problem as if it's happening to someone else. Suddenly, the answer becomes clearer.

3. Brainstorm First, Judge Later

Most people kill their own solutions before they're even born. They think of an idea and instantly dismiss it: "Nah, that won't work." Don't do that! Just list down every possible solution, even the crazy ones. The best solutions often come from unexpected places.

4. Focus on What You CAN Control

Some things are just out of your hands. If it's raining, you can't stop the rain. But you can grab an umbrella. The key is to shift focus from complaining to controlling what's controllable.

5. Take Immediate Action

A solution is useless if you don't act on it. Even a small step forward is better than waiting for a perfect plan. Start moving, adjust on the way.

Why This Mindset Changes Everything

A solution-oriented person is powerful. Why? Because they never feel truly stuck. They become confident, resourceful, and, most importantly, unstoppable.

And here's the best part—once you start thinking this way, people notice. You become that go-to person who always has an answer. Opportunities come knocking. Life gets easier.

So, the next time life throws a problem your way, don't ask "Why me?" Ask, "Okay, how do I fix this?"

That's the mindset shift that changes everything.

Mindset & Success Lessons from Highly Successful People

Hmmm... so you wanna know what makes highly successful people different? Wow, great question! But first, let me ask you something—ever seen someone sipping coffee, looking all serious, and typing furiously on their laptop in a cafe? Yeah, they look successful, right? Plot twist—they might just be writing an angry email to customer support because their pizza arrived cold. Hahaha!

See, real success isn't about looking successful; it's about having the right mindset. Let's break it down- of course!

---

1. Fail Fast, Fail Often – Like a Pro!

Oh shit! You failed? Damnnn... welcome to the club of legends! Steve Jobs got kicked out of Apple. J.K. Rowling got rejected 12 times. Even Michael Jordan was cut from his high school basketball team. And here we are, crying over one bad day. Hahaha, chill! The faster you fail, the faster you learn. So, next time you mess up? Say, "Wow! Another step closer to succes

---

2. Confidence is Just a Trick (Fake It Till You Make It!)

You think all successful people are super confident? Nah! They're just good at faking it. Elon Musk? He once said he thought Tesla would fail. But did he walk around saying, "Guys, I don't know what I'm doing"?? Nope! He walked like a boss and figured things out on the way. So next time you doubt yourself, just pretend you're a genius and walk in like you own the place. Boom!

---

3. Time Is Money – Use It Well!

Jeff Bezos and you have the same 24 hours. Difference? He used his hours wisely, and you? You just spent 2 hours watching cat videos. DAMN IT! Successful people value their time like gold. So, next time you waste time, just remember—someone else is using that same time to build their dream. Ouch!

---

4. Solve Problems, Don't Cry Over Them!

Highly successful people don't complain. They fix things. Mark Zuckerberg didn't say, "Ugh, I wish there was a better way to connect people." No, he BUILT Facebook. Every problem has a solution—find it!

Final Thought:

Success isn't about luck or talent. It's about mindset, baby! Work on it, be consistent, and keep going. And the next time someone says, "You can't do it," just smile and say, "Hmmm... watch me!"

"Your Move:"

Think about one negative belief you have about yourself.

Now, replace it with a positive belief and act on it.

Your mindset is your superpower. Train it, use it, and watch how your life changes.

VIII

THE FUTURE CALL

We always think we have time. Right? Tomorrow, next week, next year. There's always another chance.

That's what Rahul believed too. A college student with big dreams but little action. He spent most of his time scrolling through social media, watching videos, making grand plans in his head—but never actually starting anything.

"Tomorrow," he'd say. "I'll do it tomorrow."

But somehow, tomorrow never came.

That evening, he lay on his bed, mindlessly scrolling through his phone. The glow of the screen reflected in his tired eyes. That's when it happened.

A call.

Unknown number.

Rahul frowned. Normally, he ignored such calls. But something about this one felt... different.

His phone screen flashed a name.

Future Rahul.

His eyebrows furrowed. **A prank?** He hesitated, then answered.

"Hello?"

A deep, familiar voice responded, "Rahul, listen carefully. I don't have much time. I am you. From the future."

Rahul scoffed, rolling his eyes. "Very funny. Who is this? One of my friends trying to mess with me?"

"Rahul, stop. *You waste hours every day*, thinking you'll start later. You won't. If you don't change, I promise you, five years from now, you'll regret every second you wasted."

A strange chill ran down his spine. He sat up. "And what exactly am I supposed to regret?"

The voice sighed. "Where do I even begin? You never took your studies seriously, so you missed out on opportunities. You never built any skills, so you struggled to find a job you actually liked. You kept postponing workouts, and now your health is a mess. You pushed people away, thinking you'd reconnect later, but guess what? They moved on."

Silence.

Rahul swallowed hard. Deep down, he knew this wasn't just some prank. He wasn't doing anything meaningful with his time. He always thought he had more of it.

He hesitated. "What do I do?"

"Start. Today. Even if it's small. Study for thirty minutes. Exercise, even if it's just a walk. Apply for something, even if you feel unprepared. Just. Start."

Rahul clenched his jaw. "And what if I fail?"

The voice was firm. "You will. But failure is better than regret. You fail, you learn. You do nothing, you lose."

A lump formed in Rahul's throat. He had wasted years waiting for the perfect time. Maybe this was it.

"I'll try."

The voice softened. "Don't just try. Do it. Because if you don't, I'll call you again in five years. And trust me, you won't like what I have to say then."

Click.

The call ended.

Rahul stared at his phone, heart racing. Then, without another thought, he turned off his notifications, picked up his books, and started studying.

Just a small step. But for the first time, he was moving forward.

And from that day on, he never waited for 'tomorrow' again.

IX

ACTION CREATE MOMENTUM

Ever noticed how tired you feel before a workout but supercharged afterward? That's because energy is a byproduct of movement. When you move, your brain lights up, your body reacts, and suddenly, you're unstoppable.

The Science Behind Momentum

Momentum isn't just a physics concept that tormented us in high school. It's the secret sauce behind every major success story. Whether it's a rocket launching into space, a student acing exams, or you finally cleaning your room after months of procrastination—momentum plays a massive role. But what exactly is momentum, and why does it feel like life is on 'easy mode' once we get into the flow? Let's dive into the science behind momentum, with a sprinkle of humor, of course.

Newton Knew What He Was Talking About

Sir Isaac Newton wasn't just an apple enthusiast; he gave us the first law of motion, which basically says: *An object at rest stays at rest, and an object in motion stays in motion unless acted upon by an external force.* Now, let's translate that into real life:

If you're binge-watching Netflix on your couch, you'll probably stay there forever unless something (hunger, guilt, or your mom) forces you to move.

But if you've started working out, studying, or writing a novel, chances are you'll keep going because you're already in motion.

The hardest part? Getting started. But once you're moving, things get much easier.

The Psychological Side of Momentum

Our brains love patterns and habits. Once you repeat an action enough times, your brain automates it, making it easier to do. This is why the first five minutes of any task feel like torture, but after twenty minutes, you're cruising. Momentum builds as you engage in an activity consistently.

Your brain also releases dopamine, the "feel-good" neurotransmitter, whenever you make progress. This dopamine rush encourages you to keep going, making momentum a self-reinforcing loop.

The 'Rolling Snowball' Effect

Imagine pushing a snowball down a hill. At first, it's small and slow, but as it keeps rolling, it gets bigger and faster. That's momentum in action.

First few reps at the gym? Painful.

First 100 words of an essay? Agonizing.

First hour of waking up early? A nightmare.

But once you've done it for a while, you don't even think about it anymore. That's because momentum removes the initial friction and replaces it with speed and ease.

How To Hack Momentum To Your Advantage

Momentum doesn't just appear; you have to create it. Here's how:

1. Start Small – Don't try to overhaul your entire life in one day. Want to get fit? Do 5 push-ups. Want to write a book? Write 50 words. Small actions build momentum without overwhelming you.

2. Remove Distractions – Interruptions kill momentum. Put your phone on silent, lock your door, and tell the world you're busy.

3. Stack Your Wins – Celebrate small victories. Finished a page? Reward yourself with a high-five (even if it's to yourself).

4. Consistency Over Intensity – One intense gym session won't make you fit, but regular workouts will. The same applies to any skill or goal.

5. Create Triggers – Attach habits to existing routines. Want to start reading? Do it with your morning coffee.

Momentum in Real Life

Think of any successful person—Elon Musk, Oprah, Cristiano Ronaldo. None of them became great overnight. They started with small actions, gained momentum, and eventually reached greatness.

The same principle applies to you. Whether you're studying, working on a project, or trying to wake up early, the key is to push past the initial resistance. Because once you're in motion, nothing can stop you—except maybe an all-you-can-eat pizza buffet.

Final Thoughts

Momentum is like a superpower. It makes difficult tasks easier, helps you stay consistent, and turns effort into effortless action. The trick? Just get started. Even if it's the tiniest step, take it. Before you know it, you'll be unstoppable.

Now, stop scrolling and go do something productive! (Or at least pretend to.)

The Role of Energy and Motivation in Momentum

Momentum is like a stubborn dog that refuses to move when you want it to but suddenly drags you at full speed when you least expect it. But what fuels this unpredictable beast? Two things: Energy and Motivation. Without them, momentum is like a car without fuel—going nowhere.

Energy: The Gasoline of Action

Imagine waking up feeling like a potato. You want to do something productive, but your body is just... there. That's low energy, my friend. Without energy, even the most motivated people turn into expert procrastinators.

Energy is the physical and mental fuel that drives action. If you feel drained, no amount of motivational speeches or life-changing quotes will get you moving. You can watch all the "Hustle Hard" videos on YouTube, but if your body is screaming for sleep, you're not achieving anything.

So, *how do you increase energy levels?*

Move your body. Exercise, even a quick stretch, can make a huge difference. You don't need to be a gym freak, just don't be a couch potato 24/7.

Eat well. Junk food is like bad friends—feels good at the moment but drains you in the long run.

Sleep enough. You're not a robot (even robots need charging). Proper sleep = better energy.

Hydrate! Coffee helps, but water is the real MVP.

Motivation: The Spark That Ignites

Now, let's talk about motivation. If energy is the gasoline, motivation is the ignition spark that starts the engine. Without motivation, you'll just be sitting in your metaphorical car, full tank but going nowhere.

There are two types of motivation:

1. **Intrinsic motivation**: You do things because you genuinely want to (like binging your favorite show without anyone forcing you).

2. **Extrinsic motivation**: You do things because of rewards or pressure (like studying just to avoid failing exams).

Most people wait for motivation to magically appear. Bad news: it doesn't work like that.

The Energy-Motivation Loop

Here's the twist: *energy and motivation feed off each other.*

If you have high energy, you're more likely to feel motivated.

If you feel motivated, you naturally start doing things that increase your energy (exercise, eating well, etc.).

But if you wait for motivation before taking action, congratulations—you'll be stuck in an endless loop of "I'll start tomorrow" forever.

How to Hack This System

Since energy and motivation influence each other, you can hack the system by focusing on action first.

1. Start small: If you don't feel like working out, just put on your shoes. Once they're on, you might as well do something, right?

2. Change your environment: Feeling lazy? Stand up, change rooms, get some sunlight. Your brain will register this as a 'reset' button.

3. Use music: The right playlist can turn your mood from "I don't wanna do anything" to "LET'S GO!"

4. Accountability matters: Tell someone what you plan to do. Humans hate looking like liars.

5. Action before emotion: Don't wait until you "feel" like doing it. Start, and the feelings will follow.

Final Thoughts

Energy and motivation are partners in crime. If you can manage both, momentum becomes easier to sustain. Don't sit around waiting to 'feel ready.' Take action, even if it's small. Because once you start rolling, momentum takes over—and suddenly, you're unstoppable!

Now that we've fueled up on energy and motivation, let's talk about **breaking that initial resistance**—the biggest hurdle in momentum. Stay tuned!

Breaking the Initial Resistance

So, you've got a goal. Maybe it's hitting the gym, starting a business, writing that book, or even just waking up early without feeling like a zombie. You know what needs to be done, but there's this invisible force field holding you back. That, my friend, is **initial resistance.** It's like your brain's way of saying, "Nah, let's just stay comfortable."

Why Does Initial Resistance Exist?

Your brain is an efficiency machine. It loves routines and familiar patterns. Anything that disrupts that is seen as a threat. Think about it: if you've been binge-watching Netflix every evening for the last six months, your brain isn't going to suddenly cheer when you decide to replace that with jogging. Nope, it's going to fight you like a stubborn cat avoiding bath time.

On top of that, your mind magnifies the difficulty of starting something new. It's called the **"perceived effort" bias**—we assume things will be harder than they actually are. That's why the thought of writing 500 words seems like a Herculean task, but once you start, you're suddenly in the flow and hitting 2,000 words without realizing it.

The Sneaky Ways Resistance Shows Up

Resistance is a master of disguise. Here's how it usually sneaks into your life:

- **Procrastination** – "I'll start on Monday." (Spoiler: Monday never comes.)

- **Overthinking** – "But what if I fail? What if it's not perfect?"

- **Excuses** – "I don't have time. I need to research more. The universe isn't aligned yet."

- **Fear of Judgment** – "What if people laugh at me?"

Recognizing these signs is half the battle won.

How to Smash Through Initial Resistance Like a Pro

1. The Two-Minute Rule: Trick Your Brain into Action**

Instead of telling yourself, "I need to work out for an hour," say, "I'll just put on my workout clothes." Or, "I'll just write the first sentence of my book." More often than not, you'll end up continuing. **Getting started is 80% of the battle.**

2. Lower the Barrier to Entry**

Make the process stupidly easy. Want to read more? Keep a book on your pillow. Want to wake up early? Put your alarm across the room. Reduce friction so much that not taking action feels ridiculous.

3. Set an Ugly First Draft Rule**

Perfectionism is resistance's favorite weapon. Instead of aiming for perfect, aim for "done." Give yourself permission to suck at first. Whether it's writing, working out, or learning a new skill—just get it done. You can always refine later.

4. Use the Five-Second Rule**

Mel Robbins popularized this rule: **the moment you feel yourself hesitating, count 5-4-3-2-1 and move!** Your brain only needs a small push before it talks you out of doing something hard. Interrupt the hesitation cycle before it fully forms.

5. Create an Environment That Encourages Action**

Your surroundings shape your behavior. If you want to eat healthier, keep junk food out of sight. If you want to work out more, surround yourself with fitness-minded people. Your environment should pull you toward action, not resistance.

6. Make It a Game**

Gamify your resistance-breaking process. Track progress, reward yourself, challenge friends, or use apps that make habit-building fun. When something feels like a game, your brain is more likely to engage with it.

7. The "What's the Worst That Can Happen?" Approach**

Ask yourself, "If I try this and fail, what's the absolute worst thing that could happen?" 99% of the time, it's nothing catastrophic. You might feel embarrassed for five minutes or have to try again, but that's about it. Realizing this takes away resistance's power.

#Final Thought: Resistance Never Fully Goes Away—But You Get Stronger

Even the most successful people face resistance. The difference? They've built the habit of pushing through it quickly. The next time resistance shows up, don't negotiate with it. Recognize it for what it is and take action anyway. Your future self will thank you.

Now, stop reading and go do that thing you've been putting off. *5-4-3-2-1—GO!**

The Dopamine Effect of Progress

Ever wondered why ticking off a to-do list feels as satisfying as biting into your favorite chocolate? That's dopamine at work! This sneaky little neurotransmitter is like a tiny cheerleader in your brain, doing cartwheels every time you make progress. But wait, there's more! The better you understand dopamine's role in momentum, the more you can use it to trick yourself into unstoppable action.

The Brain's Reward System: The Original Hype Man

Your brain is wired to chase pleasure and avoid pain. That's why watching Netflix feels easier than hitting the gym. When you complete a task—whether it's making your bed or sending an email—your brain releases dopamine, rewarding you with a mini sense of accomplishment. The trick? Keep stacking small wins to keep that dopamine flowing.

Micro-Wins = Mega Motivation

You don't have to climb Mount Everest to get a dopamine boost. Tiny wins like drinking a glass of water, making a plan for the day, or even just opening that unread email can trigger it. Ever notice how productivity apps celebrate when you complete a task? That's not just for fun—it's hacking your brain chemistry!

Gamifying Your Progress

Want to keep momentum going? Turn life into a game. Give yourself points for completing tasks, set up a reward system (yes, even for adulting), and track your streaks. The more progress you see, the more motivated you'll be to keep going. Think of it like leveling up in a video game, but instead of a high score, you get a successful life.

Beware of Dopamine Traps

Social media, junk food, and binge-watching also release dopamine—but in a way that tricks your brain into feeling productive when you're actually doing nothing. The key is to be mindful of what activities truly move you forward versus just giving you a quick dopamine hit.

The Dopamine Loop: Your New Best Friend

Once you start seeing progress, your brain craves more. This is why people who exercise regularly find it easier to keep going—they're hooked on the good feeling of progress. The key to sustaining momentum? Keep feeding your brain small, consistent victories.

So, the next time you feel stuck, remember: your brain loves progress. Feed it tiny wins, and soon enough, you'll be riding a dopamine-fueled wave of unstoppable momentum!

How Environment Affects Your Action Level

Ever wondered why you feel super productive in a library but turn into a couch potato in your bedroom? Or why a gym with blasting motivational music makes you want to lift like The Rock, but working out at home makes you suddenly remember you need a snack? That's because your environment is like an invisible remote control for your brain—it either presses the "Get Things Done" button or the "Let's Just Chill" button.

Your surroundings play a massive role in how you act, and if you're struggling to get things done, your environment might be working against you. Let's break it down into the ways your surroundings influence your action levels and how you can tweak them to work in your favor.

1. The Power of Cues: Your Brain is a Sponge

Your brain is constantly picking up cues from the environment. If you've ever walked into a movie theater and immediately craved popcorn (even when you weren't hungry), that's your brain responding to an environmental cue. The same principle applies to productivity. If your workspace is messy, your brain gets the "chaotic" signal and struggles to focus. If your phone is lying next to you, lighting up every two seconds, your brain prioritizes scrolling over studying.

Fix it:

Designate a work-only space. Even if it's just a corner of your room, let your brain associate that area with productivity.

Remove distractions. Keep your phone out of sight when working.

Introduce cues that trigger action—like keeping a book on your desk to remind you to read.

2. The People Around You: The Energy You Absorb

Ever noticed how spending time with lazy people makes you lazier, while hanging around ambitious folks makes you want to step up your game? That's because humans are social creatures—we absorb the energy of those around us.

Fix it:

Surround yourself with action-oriented people. If you can't physically be around them, follow inspiring people online, read their books, or listen to their podcasts.

If your environment is full of distractions (like a house full of loud siblings), invest in noise-canceling headphones or work in a café or library.

3. The Digital Environment: Your Virtual Surroundings Matter Too

Your phone, laptop, and online spaces are as much a part of your environment as your physical surroundings. If your social media feed is full of meme pages and endless reels, guess what? Your brain will crave scrolling instead of action.

Fix it:

Curate your social media feed. Follow people who inspire you to take action.

Use website blockers to prevent distractions when working.

Declutter your desktop—yes, that means closing the 57 tabs you've had open for weeks.

4. The Power of Colors, Lighting, and Sounds

Ever wondered why fast-food restaurants use red and yellow? Those colors make you feel hungry and impatient. Similarly, different colors, lighting, and sounds affect your productivity. A dimly lit room with dull colors can make you feel sleepy, while a bright, well-lit workspace can make you feel energized.

Fix it:

If possible, work near natural light. It boosts mood and focus.

Use colors wisely—blue and green enhance focus, while red and yellow increase energy.

Play background music or white noise if it helps you focus.

5. Temperature and Comfort: Finding the Sweet Spot

Too cold, and you'll spend more time shivering than working. Too hot, and you'll feel sluggish. Your brain works best at an optimal temperature—typically around 22-25°C (72-77°F).

Fix it:

Adjust the temperature in your workspace to find what works best for you.

If your chair or desk is uncomfortable, you'll keep shifting around instead of focusing. Invest in a comfortable setup if you can.

6. The "Environmental Reset" Hack

If you've been stuck in a rut, sometimes changing your environment can reset your productivity. That's why people who go to coffee shops to work often get more done.

Fix it:

If you're feeling unproductive, change locations. Move to a different room, a café, or even an outdoor space.

Rearrange your workspace to give it a fresh feel.

Clean up your surroundings—cluttered space, cluttered mind.

Final Thoughts: Make Your Environment Work for You

You don't need superhuman willpower to be productive—you just need to set up an environment that naturally nudges you toward action. Small tweaks in your surroundings can have a huge impact on your motivation and productivity.

So, take a look around. Is your environment setting you up for success or dragging you down? Time to optimize it and watch your action levels skyrocket!

The 5-Second Rule for Instant Action

We've all been there. You know exactly what you need to do, but your brain starts negotiating like a lazy lawyer—"Maybe later," "Tomorrow will be better," or the classic, "Just five more minutes on my phone." Boom! The moment is gone, and you're back in the cycle of procrastination. Well, my friend, it's time to meet your new best friend: The 5-Second Rule.

What Is the 5-Second Rule?

No, it's not about dropping food on the floor and eating it before germs take over (though, let's be honest, we all follow that one too). This 5-Second Rule, coined by Mel Robbins, is a psychological hack to break hesitation and take action before your brain convinces you otherwise.

It's simple: The moment you have an instinct to act on something important, you count down—5, 4, 3, 2, 1—then move. No overthinking. No excuses. Just action.

Why Does It Work?

Our brain is a master at avoiding discomfort. It LOVES to keep us in our comfort zone, wrapped in a cozy blanket of Netflix and snacks. But the 5-Second Rule interrupts this process. It stops the brain from overanalyzing and engages the prefrontal cortex—the part responsible for decision-making and action.

By counting backward, you create a sense of urgency. Your mind doesn't have time to come up with excuses, and before you know it, you're already doing the thing you were avoiding.

How to Use It in Real Life

Getting Out of Bed: Alarm rings. Instead of hitting snooze, count 5-4-3-2-1 and jump up like a superhero.

Going to the Gym: You're lying on the couch, contemplating if fitness is even worth it. 5-4-3-2-1—get up, put on your shoes, and step out the door before your mind protests.

Speaking Up: Got an idea in a meeting? Feeling shy? 5-4-3-2-1—speak before your brain convinces you to stay silent.

Breaking Procrastination: Need to study, work, or start that project? 5-4-3-2-1—just start, even if it's for five minutes.

The Science Behind It

Studies show that hesitation activates the stress response in the brain. The longer we wait, the more anxious we feel, and the more likely we are to talk ourselves out of action. The 5-Second Rule prevents this delay, creating a mental shortcut to bypass fear and self-doubt.

But What If I Don't Feel Like It?

Ah, the golden question! Here's the secret: You will never feel like it. The motivation fairy isn't coming. The only way to feel motivated is to take action first. Action leads to progress, and progress fuels motivation.

Common Excuses & How to Shut Them Down

"I'll do it later." → Nope. 5-4-3-2-1, do it now.

"I need more time to think." → Thinking won't change anything. Action will.

"I don't feel ready." → You'll never be fully ready. Start anyway.

"What if I fail?" → What if you succeed? You'll never know unless you try.

Final Thoughts

The 5-Second Rule is like a magic spell for productivity. It won't make things easy, but it will make them possible. Next time you find yourself hesitating, don't wait. Count down. Move. Change your life, five seconds at a time.

The Snowball Effect of Taking the First Step

Ever tried to push a giant snowball down a hill? No? Well, let's imagine it! At first, it barely moves. You huff, you puff, you push, and it grudgingly starts rolling. But then—boom! It picks up speed, growing bigger and faster with every turn. That, my friend, is exactly how momentum works in real life. Taking the first step is like giving that snowball its first push. It might be small, it might feel insignificant, but once it gets rolling, there's no stopping it!

Why is the First Step So Hard?

You know that moment when you stare at your to-do list, willing it to do itself? That's the "before" phase of momentum. Your brain is in overthinking mode, convincing you that everything is too big, too complex, or too exhausting. Welcome to paralysis by analysis!

The first step feels hard because:

1. Your brain loves comfort. It doesn't want change. Change means effort, and effort means potential failure (or worse—sweat!).

2. Fear of imperfection. What if you mess up? What if you start and realize you're terrible at it? Congratulations, your inner perfectionist just built a mental wall taller than Everest.

3. You overestimate effort. You think, "This will take hours," when in reality, it probably won't. The hardest part is just starting.

The First Step is the Smallest—But the Most Powerful

Newton had it right: an object at rest stays at rest. But the moment you apply force (aka action), things start happening. The tiniest effort in the right direction can set off a chain reaction.

Want to get fit? Just put on your gym shoes and walk for five minutes.

Want to write a book? Open a blank document and type one sentence.

Want to clean your room? Just pick up one sock.

Sounds silly, right? But here's the magic: Once you start, you're way more likely to keep going.

Momentum Feeds on Itself

Ever noticed how one productive action leads to another? You decide to clean your desk, then suddenly, you're rearranging your entire room like a professional organizer. It's the same with every goal in life. The energy from one small action fuels the next.

Day 1: You write a single paragraph.

Day 5: You're halfway through a chapter.

Day 30: You have an entire book draft!

This snowball effect is how habits are built. The more you do something, the easier it gets.

How to Push Your Own Snowball

Now that we've established how powerful the first step is, let's get practical. How do you make that first push easier?

1. Shrink the Task

If something feels overwhelming, make it smaller. Instead of "I need to work out for an hour," say, "I'll do 5 push-ups." Once you do 5, you'll probably do 10. And then maybe 15. Boom! Snowball effect.

2. Use the 2-Minute Rule

Stolen from productivity genius David Allen, the rule is simple: If something takes less than 2 minutes, do it immediately. No thinking, no hesitation—just action.

3. Commit to Just One Step

Instead of saying "I have to finish this entire project," tell yourself, "I'll just start." Once you start, your brain will hate leaving it unfinished.

4. Remove Decision Fatigue

Set yourself up for success by making decisions in advance. If you want to work out, lay out your clothes the night before. If you want to write, decide what topic you'll tackle first.

5. Reward Progress

Even tiny wins deserve celebration. Finished your first page? Treat yourself to a coffee. Made it to the gym? High-five yourself in the mirror (or, you know, just smile).

Why This Works Every Time

Once you take action, your brain rewires itself. You shift from an "I can't" mindset to an "I did it!" mindset. The more wins you collect—no matter how small—the more confident you become. And confidence? That's the fuel that keeps the snowball rolling.

So next time you're stuck staring at your to-do list, overwhelmed by everything you could be doing, remember this: Just take the first step. The snowball effect will handle the rest.

Ready? 3...2...1... Push!

How to Sustain Momentum Long Term

Alright, you've taken the first step, built some momentum, and you're feeling like an unstoppable force of nature. But wait—how do you keep this momentum going long term? Because let's be real, enthusiasm fizzles out faster than New Year's resolutions. Let's go with a dash of humor, because, well, life is already too serious.

1. Set the Right Kind of Goals (Not the Over-Ambitious Monster Ones)

Listen, we all love dreaming big. "I'll hit the gym every day for the next year." Spoiler alert: You won't. The key is to set goals that are ambitious but sustainable. Instead of saying, "I'll become a millionaire in six months," try, "I'll save and invest consistently for five years." Sustainable goals prevent burnout and keep you on track.

2. Consistency Beats Intensity (Every. Single. Time.)

Ever heard of the "tortoise and the hare" story? The hare goes full throttle and then crashes; the tortoise takes small, steady steps and wins. Be the tortoise. When trying to sustain momentum, it's better to do a little every day rather than a lot once in a blue moon. If you write one page daily, you'll have a book in a year. If you work out three times a week, you'll be in great shape over time. Slow and steady doesn't just win the race—it makes sure you don't pass out halfway.

3. Make It Easy for Yourself (Hack the System)

Why do we struggle to sustain momentum? Because we make things hard for ourselves. If you want to eat healthily, keep healthy snacks within reach. If you want to wake up early, put your alarm across the room (so you can't snooze it 17 times). If you want to work out, lay out your gym clothes the night before. The easier you make the process, the less likely you are to quit.

4. Reward Yourself (But Not with Cake Every Time)

If you've been crushing your goals, give yourself a little treat—watch your favorite show, take a short trip, buy yourself something nice. Just don't fall into the trap of rewarding yourself in ways that set you back. (e.g., "I worked out for a week, so I deserve a whole pizza." See how that doesn't work?) Reward smartly, people.

5. Keep the Fire Alive (Avoid Boredom Like It's the Plague)

Boredom is momentum's biggest enemy. The moment things start feeling stale, switch it up. If you're working out, try new exercises. If you're building a business, test new ideas. If you're studying, experiment with different learning techniques. The more engaged you are, the longer you'll stay in the game.

6. Surround Yourself with the Right People (Momentum is Contagious)

Have you ever noticed how motivated you feel when hanging around ambitious people? And how lazy you get when you're surrounded by couch potatoes? Your environment shapes your momentum. Surround yourself with people who push you to do better, and avoid those who drain your energy with negativity and bad habits.

7. Track Your Progress (Because Seeing Growth is Addictive)

Nothing kills motivation faster than feeling like you're going nowhere. That's why tracking progress is so important. Whether it's a journal, an app, or a spreadsheet, find a way to measure your growth. Seeing how far you've come will make you want to keep going.

8. Learn to Pivot, Not Quit

Life happens. Maybe your plan doesn't work out exactly as expected. That doesn't mean you should stop—it means you should adjust. If your workout routine isn't showing results, tweak it. If your business strategy isn't working, refine it. The key to long-term momentum isn't perfection—it's adaptation.

9. Stay Accountable (Because We're All a Little Lazy Without It)

Tell someone about your goals—whether it's a friend, mentor, or even social media. When other people know what you're working on, you're less likely to quit. Nobody wants to be that person who loudly announces they're starting something and then disappears two weeks later.

10. Don't Rely on Motivation (It's a Fickle Friend)

Let's get one thing straight: Motivation is unreliable. Some days you'll feel like a productivity beast, and other days, getting out of bed will feel like climbing Mount Everest. This is why discipline > motivation. Build habits that keep you going, even when motivation is nowhere to be found.

11. Remember Why You Started (Because the Middle is the Hardest Part)

The beginning is exciting, and the end is rewarding—but the middle? That's where most people quit. When things get tough, remind yourself why you started in the first place. Visualize your end goal. Imagine how good it will feel to achieve what you set out to do.

Final Thoughts: Ride the Wave, Don't Fight It

Momentum isn't something you force—it's something you ride. When you feel the wave, go with it. When you hit a rough patch, don't panic. Adjust, stay consistent, and keep moving forward. Over time, you'll realize that sustaining momentum isn't about being perfect; it's about showing up, day after day, and refusing to quit.

So, are you ready to keep the momentum alive? Let's go!

How to Restart Momentum After a Break

So, you were on fire, getting things done like a productivity ninja, and then—BAM!—you took a break.

Maybe it was a well-deserved vacation, a "quick" Netflix binge that turned into a week-long series marathon, or just life getting in the way. And now, getting back into the groove feels like trying to push a broken-down car uphill. Sounds familiar? Don't worry, restarting momentum is an art, and I've got the brush and paint for you.

Step 1: Accept That Breaks Happen (And That's Okay!)

First things first, stop beating yourself up for taking a break. You're not a machine (unless you are, in which case, impressive). Breaks are part of the process. Instead of guilt-tripping yourself into inertia, acknowledge the pause and move on. Even the most successful people take breaks—they just don't let those breaks turn into indefinite vacations.

Step 2: Start Small – Like, Really Small

One of the biggest mistakes people make when trying to restart momentum is thinking they have to dive back in at full speed. Nope. That's like expecting to run a marathon after sitting on your couch for a month. Instead, start ridiculously small. Write one sentence, do one push-up, answer one email—just get the ball rolling.

Step 3: Set the Bar Low (But Not Too Low)

If you aim to go from zero to hero in one day, chances are you'll burn out before you even begin. Set small, achievable goals that push you just enough. For example, if you were writing a book but took a month off, don't aim to write 5,000 words on your first day back. Start with 500, then increase it gradually.

Step 4: Reignite the 'Why'

Why were you doing this in the first place? Was it for financial freedom? Self-improvement? To prove your ex wrong? Whatever your motivation was, remind yourself of it. Momentum is easier to regain when you have a strong reason behind your actions.

Step 5: Eliminate the "Re-Start" Resistance

The hardest part of restarting momentum is overcoming that mental resistance. Your brain is like, "Eh, let's just keep relaxing." The trick? Make the first step stupidly easy. If you want to start working out again, just put on your workout clothes. If you want to start reading again, just open the book. Taking that first step makes the next steps inevitable.

Step 6: Use the '5-Second Rule'

Mel Robbins' famous 5-second rule states that if you have an instinct to act on a goal, you must do it within five seconds before your brain convinces you otherwise. So, the next time you think, "I should start working again," count down—5, 4, 3, 2, 1—AND GO!

Step 7: Leverage the Power of Environment

Your environment plays a massive role in your ability to restart momentum. If you're trying to get back to studying but your desk looks like a post-apocalyptic wasteland, clean it up. If you want to work out, set your shoes and clothes out the night before. Make the right action the easy action.

Step 8: Track Progress, But Gently

Don't obsess over tracking every little thing, but do keep a simple record of your actions. A checklist, a habit tracker, or even a "Did I do something today?" journal can keep you accountable. The goal is to build consistency without overwhelming yourself.

Step 9: Rebuild the Streak

Ever noticed how once you do something two or three days in a row, it gets easier? That's because momentum builds on itself. Use this to your advantage. Set a goal to keep your streak alive for at least a few days, and soon enough, you'll be back to full speed.

Step 10: Reward Yourself (Strategically)

Bribing yourself works. If you restart momentum and complete a small milestone, treat yourself to something nice—but don't overdo it. Finishing one workout doesn't mean you deserve an entire pizza. (Okay, maybe just a slice.) The idea is to associate progress with positive reinforcement.

Step 11: Don't Wait for Motivation—Create It

Waiting for motivation is like waiting for a unicorn to deliver your morning coffee. Motivation comes after action, not before it. Start taking small steps, and soon enough, the motivation will catch up.

Conclusion: Momentum Loves Action

Restarting momentum after a break isn't about making grand gestures—it's about taking small, consistent actions that add up. Start tiny, build gradually, and before you know it, you'll be back in full swing. Now, go take that first step—seriously, right now. 5, 4, 3, 2, 1... GO!

"Your Move:"

Stop reading. Right now. Take one small action toward your goal. Just one. Do it.

Momentum is waiting. Are you ready to unleash it?

X

THE 70% RULE [JEFF BEZOS]

Success isn't about waiting for the perfect moment; it's about making the best decision with the information you have. That's exactly what Jeff Bezos, the founder of Amazon, believes in. His 70% Rule is a game-changer, a mindset shift that separates the action-takers from the overthinkers.

The Origin of the 70% Rule

Imagine you're standing in front of a buffet, and you see a hundred different dishes. Your stomach grumbles, but your brain freezes. Should you take the pasta? Or maybe the sushi? Oh, wait! There's biryani too! And just like that, instead of enjoying a meal, you spend half an hour staring at the options, paralyzed by choice.

Welcome to the world of decision fatigue, the silent productivity killer.

Now, what if I told you that the world's best decision-makers—whether in business, sports, or even the military—don't wait for 100% certainty before making a move? They operate on what's known as the 70% Rule. The idea is simple: If you have 70% of the necessary information, confidence, or resources, you go for it. You don't wait for perfection; you act.

But where did this rule come from? And why does it work?

The Military Origins

The 70% Rule wasn't born in a cozy boardroom; it came straight from high-stakes environments where life and death decisions are made in seconds.

One of the most famous proponents of this rule was General Colin Powell, the former U.S. Secretary of State and a four-star general. He famously said:

> "Use the 40-70 rule. Once the information is in the 40% to 70% range, go with your gut. Don't wait for 100%, because by then, someone else has already acted."

In war, waiting for complete certainty often means waiting too long. By the time a soldier gathers 100% of the information, the enemy has already moved, and the opportunity is lost.

But this principle isn't just for generals barking orders on a battlefield. It applies to everything—entrepreneurship, personal growth, even choosing what to eat at a buffet (seriously, just pick something!).

Why 70%? Why Not 50% or 90%?

Good question! Let's break it down:

Less than 50%: You're basically guessing. Acting on such little information is like jumping out of a plane without checking if your parachute is packed. (Hint: That's bad.)

70%: This is the sweet spot. You're not blindly leaping, but you're also not stuck in overthinking mode. It's enough information to make an educated decision while keeping up the momentum.

90% or more: By the time you reach 90%, the world has already moved forward. The business deal is gone, the opportunity has passed, and the buffet has run out of biryani (a true tragedy).

Evolution and Decision-Making

Ever wondered why humans evolved to make fast decisions instead of perfect ones?

Back in the caveman days, our ancestors didn't have the luxury of analyzing everything for hours. If they saw something rustling in the bushes, they had two choices:

1. Wait for more information – This could mean standing still and checking if the rustling was a rabbit or a tiger.

2. Act quickly – Assume it's a tiger and run.

The ones who chose option 2 survived longer. Over thousands of years, this instinct was wired into us: When in doubt, act.

Fast forward to today, and we don't deal with tigers anymore (well, unless you work in a jungle), but the decision-making process remains the same. Whether it's investing in stocks, launching a startup, or even choosing a Netflix series, waiting for too much certainty often leads to missing the boat.

The 70% Rule in Everyday Life

Still not convinced? Here's how the 70% Rule applies to real-life situations:

Job Interviews: If you meet 70% of the job requirements, apply. Most hiring managers care more about potential than perfection.

Dating: If you find someone who matches 70% of what you're looking for, give them a chance. (Waiting for a 100% perfect partner? Good luck staying single forever.)

Starting a Business: You don't need the perfect business plan. If you have 70% of the knowledge and resources, launch. You'll figure out the rest as you go.

Learning a Skill: If you understand 70% of a new topic, start applying it. The rest will come with experience.

Final Thoughts

The 70% Rule isn't about recklessness. It's about calculated action. It tells us that waiting for perfection is just another form of procrastination.

If you keep waiting for the "perfect moment" to start, you'll be waiting forever. The real winners in life, business, and even buffets are those who take action before they feel 100% ready.

So, the next time you find yourself overthinking, ask:

"Do I have at least 70% of what I need?"

If the answer is yes, go for it. The remaining 30%? You'll figure it out along the way.

How the 70% Rule Speeds Up Decision Making

Decision-making is a tricky business. Too fast, and you might regret it. Too slow, and you might miss the opportunity. Enter the 70% Rule—a practical, no-nonsense approach to making decisions faster and more effectively. It's a concept that even top CEOs, military strategists, and entrepreneurs swear by. But how exactly does it work, and why is it such a game-changer?

The Paralysis of Perfection

We've all been there—staring at a menu for 20 minutes, scrolling endlessly on Netflix, or debating whether to send that risky text. The truth is, we often overcomplicate decisions. Our brain tells us that we need all the information before acting. But in reality, waiting for 100% certainty is a one-way ticket to Decision Paralysis Land. And guess what? The train has no return ticket.

The 70% Rule states that once you have about 70% of the information needed, you should make the decision and move forward. Why? Because waiting for 100% certainty often means waiting forever—or at least until the opportunity passes.

Why 70%? [Quick Recape]

Why not 60% or 80%? The magic of 70% is that it balances risk and reward. At 70%, you have enough information to make an informed decision, but you're not wasting time chasing perfection. This threshold is used by military leaders, like former U.S. Secretary of Defense Colin Powell, who famously applied this rule to battlefield decision-making. And if it's good enough for life-and-death situations, it's probably good enough for deciding whether to launch a project, hire a candidate, or buy that expensive gadget.

Faster Decisions = Faster Results

One of the biggest benefits of the 70% Rule is that it speeds up the entire decision-making process. Instead of overanalyzing every minor detail, you:

1. Gather just enough information – Not too little that you're shooting in the dark, but not too much that you get stuck in analysis paralysis.

2. Make the call – Trust that 70% is enough, take the leap, and execute.

3. Adapt as needed – If new information comes up, adjust your strategy. After all, most decisions are reversible.

The Business Edge

Amazon's Jeff Bezos is a huge advocate of the 70% Rule. He believes that waiting for 90% or more certainty is a recipe for stagnation. Amazon thrives on fast decision-making, and its success is proof that speed matters. In business, opportunities come and go in the blink of an eye. If you hesitate too long, your competitors will snatch them away.

Bezos calls this a "Day 1" mentality—making decisions with the urgency of a startup, even when you're a trillion-dollar company. If you're wrong? No worries. Course correct and move on. But indecision? That's the real killer.

Personal Decision-Making and the 70% Rule

This rule isn't just for business leaders—it applies to everyday life. Consider:

Buying a house – You'll never have all the details. If it checks 70% of your boxes, go for it.

Choosing a career path – If it aligns with 70% of your interests and goals, take the plunge.

Dating & relationships – No one's perfect. If a person meets 70% of your criteria, they're worth a shot.

But What If You're Wrong?

Ah, the million-dollar question. Here's the deal—mistakes are inevitable. The 70% Rule doesn't promise perfection; it promises momentum. A wrong decision can be corrected. But a delayed decision? That's just an opportunity lost.

Final Thoughts

Speed is power, and the 70% Rule is your secret weapon for faster, more effective decision-making. Whether in business, personal life, or high-stakes situations, this rule keeps you moving forward without getting stuck in the endless loop of 'What ifs?' So, the next time you're agonizing over a decision, ask yourself—do you have 70% of the information? If yes, make the call and never look back.

70% Rule vs. Analysis Paralysis

The Great Battle: 70% Rule vs. Overthinking Disorder

Imagine this: You're standing in front of two doors. Behind one is success, behind the other—well, more decisions to make. But here's the catch: you have only 70% of the information needed to choose. Do you walk through, or do you stand there frozen, analyzing every possible outcome like a detective in a crime thriller?

Welcome to the war between the 70% Rule and Analysis Paralysis—the epic showdown between smart decision-making and getting stuck in an infinite loop of "what-ifs."

What is Analysis Paralysis? (A.K.A. Overthinking Syndrome)

Analysis Paralysis is that evil twin of decision-making where you overanalyze things so much that you end up doing...absolutely nothing. You weigh pros and cons until your brain hurts, create ten different spreadsheets, watch 15 YouTube videos, and read 100 Reddit threads. In the end? Zero action.

It's like standing in a restaurant, staring at the menu for hours, afraid to order because—what if the pasta isn't good? What if the pizza has too much cheese? (Okay, that's a dumb question. There's no such thing as too much cheese.)

Enter: The 70% Rule

On the other side, the 70% Rule is like that chill friend who says, "Bro, just go for it." The rule states that if you have 70% of the information needed, it's enough to take action. You don't need 100% certainty—because, let's be honest, 100% certainty rarely exists.

It's what successful people use to move fast and make decisions efficiently. Instead of waiting for the "perfect" moment (spoiler: it doesn't exist), they take calculated action with the information they have.

Jeff Bezos swears by this. He believes that waiting for 90-100% information means you're too late. In his words, "If you wait for 90% certainty, you've probably waited too long.

Why Analysis Paralysis is Dangerous

1. Missed Opportunities: The world moves fast. If you take too long to decide, you might miss the boat (or the

rocket, if you're Elon Musk).

2. Mental Exhaustion: Overthinking drains your brain. It's like running a marathon inside your head but never actually moving forward.

3. Fear of Failure Increases: The more you think, the scarier the decision seems. Over time, this makes you hesitant to take even small risks.

4. Procrastination: Analysis Paralysis is the perfect excuse to keep delaying things. "I'm still researching" sounds smarter than "I'm scared to decide."

How to Overcome Analysis Paralysis with the 70% Rule

1. Set a Decision Deadline

If you give yourself unlimited time to decide, you'll never stop thinking. Set a deadline: "I will decide within 24 hours." This forces you to make a move.

2. Focus on Action, Not Perfection

Perfection is an illusion. Instead of asking, "Is this the best decision?" ask, "Is this a good enough decision to start?"

3. Trust Experience, Not Just Information

You don't always need more data. Trust your intuition and past experiences. If you've made similar decisions before, go with your gut.

4. Limit Your Research Time

Instead of researching endlessly, set a limit: "I'll spend 2 hours researching, then I'll decide." More research doesn't always lead to better decisions.

5. Start Small, Then Adjust

Take small steps and tweak things as you go. If you realize you're wrong, pivot. Small mistakes are easier to fix than no action at all.

The Mindset Shift: 70% is Enough

The biggest shift? Understanding that perfect decisions don't exist. Even the best CEOs, entrepreneurs, and leaders don't have 100% certainty. They just make the best decision they can with what they know—and they MOVE.

Think of life like a GPS. You start driving, and if you take the wrong turn, it recalculates. The key is to start moving.

Final Thoughts: Choose Wisely

So, are you going to wait forever for the "perfect" moment? Or are you going to trust the 70% Rule and take action?

Remember: Action beats perfection. Progress beats overthinking.

Now, go order that pizza. You know you want to.

The 70% Rule in Business Strategy: Speed, Efficiency, and Success

In the ever-changing world of business, decisions need to be made fast. You can't afford to sit in a conference room for months debating the color of the 'Buy Now' button on your website. Enter the 70% Rule—a strategy embraced by some of the most successful business leaders, including Jeff Bezos. This principle suggests that you don't need to have 100% certainty before making a decision; instead, 70% of the necessary information is often enough to move forward. But why does this work so well, and how can it be applied effectively in business strategy? Let's break it down.

Why Business Can't Wait for 100% Certainty

In an ideal world, every business decision would be made with perfect information. But in reality, waiting for complete certainty is a death sentence for progress. By the time you reach 100% confidence, the opportunity has likely passed, your competitor has already taken the lead, and you're left analyzing outdated data.

The business landscape is dynamic—market trends shift, customer behaviors change, and new technologies disrupt industries overnight. The 70% Rule allows companies to move swiftly, capitalize on opportunities, and maintain agility in uncertain environments.

Speed is a Competitive Advantage

One of the most significant benefits of the 70% Rule in business strategy is speed. Companies that make decisions quickly can test ideas, iterate, and improve while their competition is still stuck in analysis paralysis. Amazon, for example, doesn't wait for every possible piece of data before launching new products or features. Instead, they use available information to take action, collect real-world feedback, and refine their approach accordingly.

The faster you make decisions, the faster you can learn from your mistakes. And in business, learning quickly is often more valuable than being right every single time.

Risk Management: Calculated, Not Reckless

Some might argue that making decisions with only 70% of the data sounds risky. And they're not wrong—it is a risk. But it's a calculated risk, which is what makes it so effective. The key is to develop a framework that balances bold decision-making with the ability to pivot when necessary.

A few ways businesses apply the 70% Rule while managing risk include:

Prototyping before full-scale production: Launch a minimum viable product (MVP) to test market response before committing to mass production.

A/B testing in marketing: Instead of debating endlessly about an ad campaign, run two versions and let real data determine the winner.

Incremental investment: Instead of an all-or-nothing approach, invest in small increments and adjust based on results.

The 70% Rule in Decision-Making Frameworks

Great business strategies rely on decision-making frameworks that prevent stagnation. Many successful companies embed the 70% Rule into their culture using methods like:

Agile Methodology: Focused on quick iterations and continuous improvement, this approach thrives on fast decision-making with available data.

Fail Fast, Learn Faster: A mindset that encourages rapid testing and adaptation, even if initial results aren't perfect.

Data-Driven But Not Data-Paralyzed: Use analytics and metrics to inform decisions, but don't let endless reports stall action.

Examples of the 70% Rule in Action

Apple's Product Launches: Apple doesn't wait for every possible bug to be fixed before launching a new iPhone. They launch, collect feedback, and roll out software updates to improve user experience over time.

Tesla's Innovation Approach: Elon Musk's companies often deploy products before they are fully polished. Tesla vehicles receive over-the-air software updates, improving performance after customers have already purchased them.

Netflix's Content Strategy: Instead of relying on 100% perfect data to predict a show's success, Netflix greenlights shows based on partial data trends, audience engagement, and content experiments.

Common Mistakes to Avoid

While the 70% Rule is powerful, it's not a free pass to make reckless decisions. Here are some common pitfalls businesses should avoid:

Ignoring Critical Data: Some decisions—like major financial investments or compliance-related matters—may require more than 70% certainty.

Failing to Adapt: Making a decision with 70% information is good, but failing to adjust when new data emerges is a disaster.

Using It as an Excuse for Poor Planning: Speed should not come at the cost of strategy. A poorly thought-out decision, even if made quickly, can lead to long-term problems.

Final Thoughts: The 70% Rule as a Business Superpower

In today's fast-moving world, waiting for absolute certainty is often a losing strategy. The 70% Rule empowers businesses to take action, learn, and iterate faster than competitors who are stuck overanalyzing. By embracing this principle, companies can stay ahead of the curve, make smarter decisions, and ultimately drive long-term success.

So, the next time you're stuck in a never-ending strategy meeting, ask yourself—do you really need 100% certainty, or is 70% enough to take action?

Taking Calculated Risks by 70% Information

Imagine you're standing at the edge of a diving board, peering down into the deep blue pool below. You don't know if the water is warm or cold, but you do know two things: first, the pool is filled with water (thankfully), and second, other people have already jumped and survived. Do you need to test the chemical composition of the water before you take the leap? No. You just need about 70% certainty that this is a good idea.

That's the essence of taking calculated risks using 70% information. If you wait for 100% certainty, you'll probably never jump—or worse, someone else will jump before you and steal all the fun. Or, in business terms, the opportunity will vanish while you're busy overanalyzing.

Why 100% Certainty is a Mirage

The problem with waiting for 100% information is that it rarely exists. Markets fluctuate, trends shift, and new data emerges constantly. If you keep waiting for the "perfect" moment where you have all the facts, you'll be left in the dust by those who took action with just enough knowledge to move forward.

Think about the biggest business successes. Steve Jobs didn't have a 100% guarantee that the iPhone would revolutionize the world—he had a strong hunch, backed by enough data to suggest it was worth the risk. Jeff Bezos didn't wait until he had every single book cataloged before launching Amazon—he started with a hypothesis, a website, and a garage.

The 70% Rule in Action

The 70% rule suggests that once you have about 70% of the necessary information, you should act. Here's how it plays out:

1. Gather Available Data: Conduct research, analyze past trends, and consult with experts. If you were investing in a startup, you'd check their market potential, financial health, and competitor landscape.

2. Weigh the Risks: With the data in hand, assess the downside. Is the potential failure manageable? Can you pivot if things don't go as planned?

3. Make a Decision: If the upside significantly outweighs the downside and you're about 70% sure it's a good bet, move forward.

Real-Life Examples of the 70% Rule

1. Elon Musk and Tesla

When Musk decided to go all-in on electric cars, the data wasn't 100% in his favor. The EV market was tiny, infrastructure was lacking, and major automakers weren't convinced. But Musk saw a 70% chance that battery technology and government incentives would shift the tide. Today, Tesla is a trillion-dollar company.

2. Dating and Relationships

Think about choosing a life partner. Do you need to know every single detail about someone before deciding to commit? No. You need enough information—about 70%—to feel confident they're a good fit, and then you take the plunge. If you wait for a 100% guarantee that they'll never annoy you, never argue, or never leave dirty dishes in the sink, you'll be single forever.

3. Launching a Business

Many successful businesses were started on partial information. If every entrepreneur waited until they had a foolproof business plan, competitors would swoop in and take over the market. The key is knowing when you have enough data to make an educated leap.

How to Apply the 70% Rule to Your Life

1. Job Decisions

Should you take that job offer? You'll never know everything about a company before you join. But if the salary, culture, and growth opportunities align with your goals by about 70%, it's probably worth the risk.

2. Investing

No investment comes with 100% certainty. A stock might seem promising based on market research and financial trends, but unexpected events can change everything. Smart investors act when they're 70% sure, not when every possible variable is accounted for.

3. Moving to a New City

You've done your research: the cost of living is within budget, the job market is strong, and you like the vibe. Is there a chance you'll hate it? Sure. But if you're 70% sure it's a good move, it's time to pack your bags.

The Fear of Imperfection

Many people hesitate because they fear making mistakes. They think, "What if I get it wrong?" The reality is, you will get things wrong sometimes. But perfectionism often leads to inaction, which is a greater risk than making a less-than-perfect choice. Moving forward with 70% certainty beats standing still with 100% doubt.

Final Thoughts: Action Beats Hesitation

The 70% rule is a powerful tool for making faster, smarter decisions. It allows you to balance analysis with action, ensuring you don't get stuck in an endless loop of overthinking. Whether in business, relationships, or personal growth, waiting for absolute certainty is often just an excuse to delay. Life rewards those who take calculated risks.

So, the next time you're on that metaphorical diving board, remember: if you're 70% sure, it's time to jump.

Applying the 70% Rule in Daily Life

The 70% rule is not just a concept for business or investment; it can be a game-changer in everyday decision-making. Think about the times when you hesitated because you weren't 100% sure about something. Whether it's choosing a career path, making a purchase, or even deciding to move to a new city, waiting for complete certainty can lead to missed opportunities. The 70% rule offers a practical solution to this dilemma.

Making Everyday Decisions Faster

One of the biggest benefits of applying the 70% rule in daily life is that it helps you make decisions quickly without getting stuck in overthinking. For example, if you're considering buying a new phone but keep delaying the purchase because you are not sure if it's the absolute best choice, the 70% rule suggests that if you're at least 70%

sure about it, you should go ahead and make the purchase. Waiting for 100% certainty may lead to unnecessary delays and lost opportunities.

Improving Productivity and Time Management

Many people struggle with perfectionism, which leads to procrastination. The 70% rule helps break this cycle. Instead of waiting for the perfect moment or perfect conditions, you take action when you feel 70% ready. This is especially helpful in tasks like writing, studying, or preparing for a presentation. If you aim for 100% perfection, you might never get started. But with the 70% rule, you start when you feel mostly ready, and you can improve along the way.

Financial Decisions and Budgeting

When it comes to money, the 70% rule can help with budgeting and financial planning. Many experts suggest following a 70-20-10 rule, where you allocate 70% of your income for necessities, 20% for savings, and 10% for personal spending. This approach ensures financial stability while allowing flexibility for unexpected expenses.

Relationships and Social Life

Even in personal relationships, the 70% rule can be useful. When deciding whether to start a new relationship, end a toxic friendship, or even commit to a long-term partnership, waiting for complete certainty can be unrealistic. If you feel 70% confident about the decision, it may be worth taking the step and seeing how things evolve rather than waiting for a perfect scenario that may never come.

Learning New Skills and Personal Growth

People often hesitate to try new things because they feel they're not ready. Whether it's learning a new language, starting a fitness routine, or trying a new hobby, the 70%

rule encourages you to start once you feel reasonably prepared instead of waiting until you feel 100% skilled. Most of the learning happens through experience, not just preparation.

Final Thoughts

Applying the 70% rule in daily life can lead to more decisive actions, reduced stress, and increased productivity. It allows you to focus on progress over perfection and helps you make practical choices in various aspects of life, from career and finances to personal growth and relationships. Instead of waiting for complete certainty, act when you feel mostly ready—because sometimes, good enough is better than perfect.

When Not to Use the 70% Rule

Alright, listen up! The 70% rule is cool, no doubt. It helps in decision-making, productivity, and keeping things moving. But hold on—there are moments when this rule is NOT the best choice. Yeah, you heard it right. Let's dive into situations where applying the 70% rule can backfire big time.

1. Life-or-Death Situations (No Room for 30% Error!)

Imagine you're a brain surgeon, and you decide to operate with 70% accuracy. Oh shit, your patient's survival is now a gamble! Hahaha, dammit, NO! Some fields demand 100% precision—like flying a plane, nuclear safety, or even defusing a bomb. One mistake and boom—game over.

2. When You're Learning Something New

Bro, learning a skill needs patience. Imagine trying to learn a new language but stopping at 70% understanding. Hmmm... now you're stuck in a country where you can't fully communicate. Awkward, right? Mastery takes time; don't half-ass it.

3. Ethical & Moral Decisions

This one's serious. You can't be like, "I'll be 70% honest" or "I'll be 70% loyal." Oh wow, really? That's a shortcut to losing trust and credibility. When it comes to integrity, it's all or nothing.

4. Critical Business Decisions

Jeff Bezos used the 70% rule in decision-making, but not every time! Some business moves need full assurance. Imagine launching a product with only 70% testing—customers will rip you apart in reviews. Not worth the risk.

5. When It Comes to Personal Safety

Hahaha, imagine driving and saying, "I'll follow 70% of the traffic rules." Oh damn, enjoy your hospital trip! Some rules exist for a reason—mess with them, and you're in trouble.

6. When You're Setting an Example

If you're a leader, teacher, or parent, leading with 70% effort sends the wrong message. People look up to you! Give your best, or don't do it at all.

So yeah, while the 70% rule is awesome in many areas, knowing when NOT to use it is just as important. Use it wisely, or be ready for the consequences. Simple as that!

"*Your Move*"

Are you stuck waiting for everything to be perfect? Are you delaying action because of fear and uncertainty?

Look in the mirror and ask yourself: Am I waiting too long to act?

If the answer is yes, then it's time to embrace the 70% Rule and take action NOW!

XI

BURN THE BOAT NO PLAN-B

The Psychology of No Plan B

Hmmm... so you wanna talk about having no Plan B? Alright, let's get into it. No backup, no safety net, just one shot, one chance, one way forward. Sounds risky? Yeah, it is. But it's also the secret sauce behind some of the greatest success stories ever.

See, our brain is wired for safety. It craves security. That's why most people always have a backup plan. It makes them feel comfortable, like a warm blanket on a cold night. But guess what? Comfort kills ambition. When you have a Plan B, you're subconsciously telling yourself that Plan A might fail. And when failure is an option, you don't push as hard. You don't go all in. You don't BURN for success.

Ever noticed how people perform under pressure? When they HAVE to make it work, they unlock some insane levels of creativity, grit, and resilience. That's because their brain shifts into survival mode. It stops looking for easy exits and starts finding ways to win. No distractions, no excuses, just do or die.

Think about it—when your back is against the wall, you FIGHT. You dig deep, you figure things out, you break through limits you never thought you could. That's the power of having No Plan B. It forces you to commit 100% and removes the easy way out.

Of course, some people will say, "But what if I fail? What if it doesn't work?" Dude, that's the POINT. That fear of failure is what keeps you sharp, keeps you moving. Instead of worrying about failure, worry about what happens if you don't even try.

So, *what's the psychology behind No Plan B?*

Tunnel Vision: Your mind focuses purely on making Plan A work. No distractions. No side exits.

Survival Instincts Kick In: Your brain starts working at its peak because failure is NOT an option.

More Energy, More Drive: When you have no fallback, you push harder than ever before.

Fear Transforms into Power: Instead of scaring you, fear fuels you.

No Plan B isn't for the weak. It's not for those who want to "try." It's for those who have already decided, "This is happening. No matter what."

So, the real question is—are you ready to cut off the escape routes and GO ALL IN?

Historical Examples of Burning the Boats

Alright, let's dive straight in. This idea of 'burning the boats'—sounds dramatic, right? But history is filled with leaders, warriors, and risk-takers who literally and figuratively set their escape routes on fire to make sure they had no choice but to win. Let's check out some of the most badass examples of this mindset in action.

1. Hernán Cortés (1519) – The OG Boat Burner

One of the most famous stories of burning the boats comes from the Spanish conquistador Hernán Cortés. When he and his men landed in Mexico to take on the Aztec Empire, he ordered his ships to be scuttled (some say burned). Why? Because he wanted his men to know—there was no going back. They either conquered or they died trying. And guess what? They won. No retreat, no second thoughts, just full commitment.

2. Tariq bin Ziyad (711 AD) – The Warrior Who Left No Option

A similar story comes from the Islamic general Tariq bin Ziyad. When he landed in Spain with his army to take on the Visigoths, he reportedly burned his ships and told his soldiers: "The enemy is in front of you, and the sea is behind you. Fight and die with honor, or win and claim the land." The result? They fought with everything they had and took over Spain. That's what happens when you have no way out.

3. Alexander the Great (334 BC) – The Legend Who Always Moved Forward

Alexander was known for never retreating, but in one particular battle, he allegedly burned his ships after landing on Persian shores. His message to his men? "We're either conquering Persia, or we're dying here." The dude had no chill, and it worked. Persia fell, and Alexander became one of the greatest military leaders in history.

4. Julius Caesar (49 BC) – Crossing the Rubicon

Okay, so Caesar didn't exactly burn any boats, but he did something similar. When he crossed the Rubicon River with his army, he committed an irreversible act of war against Rome. There was no turning back, only victory or destruction. Spoiler alert: he won.

5. The Vikings – The Savage Warriors

The Vikings had this insane strategy where they would land on enemy shores and immediately burn their own ships. The message? They either won and took over the land, or they died trying. No retreat, no surrender, just absolute commitment. And let's be real—the Vikings were some of the most feared warriors in history for a reason.

6. South Korean CEO's Bold Move

Fast forward to modern times, and we have South Korean CEO Byung-chul Lee, the founder of Samsung. When he started, Samsung was just a small trading company. But in 1995, he made a radical decision—he literally burned 150,000 defective mobile phones to send a message to his employees: "We either make the best quality, or we're nothing." That mindset turned Samsung into one of the biggest tech giants in the world.

What's the Lesson Here?

Burning the boats is all about commitment. If you leave yourself an easy escape, your brain will always look for a way out. But when you remove the safety net, you force yourself to operate at a level you never thought possible.

So, ask yourself—what's your boat? What's the thing keeping you from going all-in? Maybe it's a backup job, a fallback plan, or even just a mindset of hesitation. Whatever it is, maybe it's time to burn it.

Your Move:

Identify one area in your life where you've been keeping a Plan B.

Ask yourself if that safety net is holding you back from giving 100%.

If it is, consider 'burning the boat' and committing fully.

No way out. Just forward. Let's go.

Survival Instinct - When You Have No Choice

Alright, so let's get real. Have you ever been in a situation where you had absolutely NO backup plan? Like, if you fail, you're done? That's survival instinct kicking in. It's that raw, primal force that drives you to do whatever it takes to stay afloat. When there's no Plan B, suddenly, Plan A isn't just a choice—it's your only damn option. And that's where magic happens.

Why Having No Choice Makes You Unstoppable

When you don't have an escape route, your mind goes into overdrive. Your brain rewires itself to find solutions, to adapt, to push beyond limits you didn't even know existed. Think about it—when do people run the fastest? When a lion is chasing them. When do they work the hardest? When their survival depends on it. That's exactly why eliminating the safety net forces you to level up like never before.

The Human Brain is Wired for Survival

Science backs this up. Our ancestors survived because their brains were tuned for fight-or-flight. They couldn't afford to have a 'fallback option' when they were out hunting. Either they caught dinner, or they starved. This same instinct still lives within us, but modern life has dulled it with comfort and options. No Plan B? That wakes up your survival mode.

Real-Life Examples of Survival Instinct

1. Elon Musk: The dude threw everything he had into Tesla and SpaceX. At one point, he had to decide whether to split his last money between the two or let one fail. He bet it all. Today? You know the answer.

2. Arnold Schwarzenegger: When he moved to America, he had nothing. No Plan B. No 'backup career'. He HAD to make it. And he did. Bodybuilding, acting, politics—the guy dominated everything because failure wasn't an option.

3. Steve Jobs: Fired from Apple, broke, and ridiculed. He could have backed off, but his survival instinct took over. He created NeXT, revolutionized Pixar, and came back stronger than ever.

The 'No Choice' Advantage

You get insanely creative – When failure isn't an option, you find solutions others miss.

Your energy skyrockets – You tap into a different level of motivation when it's do-or-die.

You eliminate distractions – Suddenly, things that used to waste your time seem irrelevant.

But Be Careful...

Going all-in doesn't mean being reckless. It means committing 100%, but also being smart about how you execute. No Plan B doesn't mean no planning at all—it means making sure Plan A is so solid that you don't NEED another option.

Your Move

1. Evaluate your current goals. Are you half-assing them because you have a safety net?

2. Find something you truly believe in. You can't go all-in on something you don't love.

3. Cut off the exit routes. Make it so that success is your only way forward.

4. Trust yourself. Humans are built for survival. Tap into that instinct, and watch yourself dominate.

No safety net? No problem. Time to go beast mode.

Why Most People Keep a Plan B and Why It's a Trap

Alright, let's be real. Almost everyone keeps a Plan B. It's like a safety net, a backup option in case things don't go as planned. But here's the catch – that very safety net might be the reason you never go all-in on Plan A. Sounds crazy? Stick with me.

The Comfort of a Plan B

Most people are wired to seek security. It's human nature. Society teaches us to be cautious:

"What if it doesn't work out?"

"You should have a backup just in case."

"Never put all your eggs in one basket."

It sounds logical, right? But the problem is, this mindset keeps you from fully committing. When you know there's something to fall back on, you don't push as hard. You don't give your 100%. And in high-stakes situations, half-hearted efforts don't cut it.

The Psychological Trap of Plan B

Let's get into the psychology of it. Having a Plan B creates an unconscious mental escape route. Your brain tells you, "Even if I fail, I have another option." Guess what happens? You don't give it your all. Your survival instincts aren't fully activated because failure isn't REALLY an option.

Think about it like this: If you had to cross a raging river and the bridge behind you collapsed, you'd figure out a way forward—no matter what. But if you knew you could turn back anytime, would you push as hard? Probably not.

The Successful People Mindset

Look at some of the most successful people in history. Many of them operated with a 'No Plan B' mentality.

Elon Musk: Went all-in on Tesla and SpaceX, even when both were near bankruptcy. If he had a backup job or another business, would he have risked everything?

Steve Jobs: Didn't build Apple while considering another company as a backup. He was all in.

Michael Jordan: Didn't think, "If basketball doesn't work, I'll do something else." He put everything into being the best.

The common pattern? Full commitment. No backup plan. Just Plan A and making it work.

The Plan B That Turns Into Plan A

Here's another trap – many times, Plan B ends up becoming the real plan. You start with ambitious goals, but as soon as obstacles hit, you start leaning towards Plan B. Before you know it, you're stuck in a life you never really wanted, just because it was the safer option.

How many people do you know who wanted to be an entrepreneur but settled for a 9-to-5? How many athletes gave up too soon and took a "safe job"? The truth is, Plan B often kills Plan A before it even has a chance to succeed.

When You Might Actually Need a Plan B

Now, before you go crazy and quit everything, let's add some balance. There are times when having a safety net is smart:

If your Plan A is financially risky, having a temporary Plan B (like a side income) makes sense.

If you have dependents relying on you, a calculated risk is better than blind risk.

If your Plan A is experimental, you might need a short-term backup plan while testing it.

But the key? Don't let Plan B become a crutch. Use it as a bridge, not a permanent residence.

Your Move

If you're serious about achieving something big, ask yourself: Do I really need a Plan B, or is it just an excuse?

Are you holding onto it because it's necessary, or because it's comfortable?

If it's just comfort, ditch it. Go all in. That's how game-changers are made.

Building a No Plan B Mindset – Practical Steps

Alright, so you've decided to go all in. No backup, no safety net, just straight-up commitment to making it work. But wait—how do you actually develop this kind of mindset? Let's break it down into real, practical steps. No fluff, just straight-to-the-point action.

1. Decide With Absolute Clarity

No half-hearted commitments. If you're even 1% doubtful, you're setting yourself up for failure. Be crystal clear about what you want. Say it out loud, write it down, visualize it—whatever works. Your brain needs to know that THIS is the only option.

2. Kill All Escape Routes

History has shown that when people eliminate all exits, they perform better. Burn the boats, delete the fallback options, remove safety nets. Why? Because when there's no way out, your mind will FIND a way to succeed. You'll think sharper, act faster, and push harder.

3. Rewire Your Brain to Love Pressure

Most people crumble under pressure. You? You need to rewire your brain to THRIVE under it. Pressure is not the enemy—it's the fuel. Every time you feel fear, doubt, or uncertainty, remind yourself: "This is where champions are made."

4. Develop an "Only Forward" Attitude

A No Plan B mindset means you don't look back. There is no "what if." There is no "maybe." You keep pushing forward, no matter what obstacles hit you. You get knocked down? You get back up. Period.

5. Surround Yourself With The Right People

This is a make-or-break step. You cannot afford to be around people who plant doubt in your mind. Find those who push you, challenge you, and believe in the same "No Plan B" philosophy. Their energy will become yours.

6. Train Relentlessly

Whatever your goal is—business, sports, art—you need to be obsessed with mastery. The more you train, the more confident you become. Confidence eliminates the need for a Plan B because you KNOW you've put in the work.

7. Accept That Failure Is Part of the Journey

No Plan B doesn't mean you won't face failures. You WILL. But failure is feedback, not a dead end. Learn, adapt, adjust, and keep moving forward. The only real failure is quitting.

8. Make It Public (Optional Power Move)

If you really want to lock yourself into the No Plan B mindset, tell people. Announce your goal. Make it public. When your reputation is on the line, you're less likely to back out. It's a psychological trick that forces you to stay committed.

9. Build Mental Toughness Daily

This mindset isn't built in a day—it's trained daily. Challenge yourself constantly. Take cold showers, push beyond your limits in workouts, wake up earlier, do something uncomfortable every day. Over time, your brain will learn to embrace discomfort instead of running from it.

10. Visualize Success, But Work Like You're Losing

You should see your success in your mind clearly, but never let that visualization make you complacent. Every single day, work as if you're at risk of losing everything. Stay hungry, stay sharp, and act like someone who has NO OTHER OPTION.

"Your Move:"

You've got the steps. Now, what are you going to do with them? Are you just going to read this and nod, or are you actually going to APPLY this mindset to your life? Remember, No Plan B means full commitment. No excuses, no exit doors, just straight-up action. Your success is waiting—go get it.

XII

WRITE YOUR OWN STORY [MADE BY ME]

What Does It Mean to Write Your Own Story?

Life is often seen as a story, but the real question is: who is writing yours? Are you following a script handed to you by society, family, or circumstances, or are you the author of your own journey?

Can a Person Truly Control Their Life?

While we may not control everything, we do have the power to shape our actions, choices, and responses. Many believe in fate or destiny, but even within those beliefs, there is room for personal decisions that influence the outcome. Writing your own story means taking responsibility for your choices and directing your life towards your desired goals.

Is Destiny Already Written, or Can We Change It?

This question has been debated for centuries. Some believe in predestined paths, while others argue that we have free will. The truth likely lies somewhere in between. We may not control every event in our lives, but we control how we respond to them. By making intentional choices, setting goals, and refusing to settle for mediocrity, we can alter the course of our lives.

Following a Path Set by Society vs. Creating Your Own

From childhood, we are given a predefined script: go to school, get a job, get married, retire. But does this path align with your personal dreams and ambitions? Writing your own story means questioning societal norms and creating a life that truly fulfills you. It means defining success on your own terms rather than accepting what others expect of you.

Ultimately, writing your own story is about empowerment. It's about taking control of your narrative, making conscious choices, and living with purpose. The pen is in your hands—how will you write your story?

The "Default Story" vs. "Custom Story"

From the moment we are born, society hands us a script. This script dictates the expected path of life:

Childhood → Education → Job → Marriage → Retirement

This is the Default Story, the one that most people follow without question. Schools, parents, and even cultural norms reinforce it, making it seem like the only way to live. But have you ever stopped to ask: Is this truly the life I want?

The truth is, most people don't question the default story. They walk the well-trodden path because it feels safe and familiar. But safety doesn't always mean fulfillment. Many people wake up one day realizing they have spent their lives following someone else's script rather than writing their own.

Now, consider the Custom Story. This is the story you create for yourself, based on your passions, beliefs, and unique desires. It doesn't follow the standard template. It is built on choice rather than expectation. Those who live a custom story design their own version of success instead of accepting society's definition.

Are you following a script written by others, or are you rewriting your own?

Breaking free from the Default Story requires courage. It means questioning long-held beliefs and stepping into uncertainty. But in that uncertainty lies the potential to live a life truly aligned with who you are.

So, ask yourself: Am I ready to break out of the cycle and start writing my own story?

Mindset Shift – The 'Made by Me' Philosophy

In life, we often believe that circumstances shape our destiny, but the truth is, we have more control than we think. The 'Made by Me' philosophy is about taking charge of our own story, shifting from a passive participant to an active creator.

"You Are the Scriptwriter of Your Life"

Most people live by a pre-written script influenced by society, family, and external expectations. But what if you took the pen into your own hands? Instead of letting life happen to you, you start crafting your own narrative. Every choice, action, and belief contributes to the story you create for yourself.

The 70% Rule – Taking Control of Your Story

Life is unpredictable, and we can't control everything. However, if 70% of circumstances are within our influence, then we have the power to rewrite our own destiny. The key is to focus on what's in our hands rather than being consumed by what we cannot change. By mastering our thoughts, actions, and responses, we can take significant control over our journey.

Burn the Boats – No Backup, No Limits

True growth happens when there is no safety net. The phrase "Burn the Boats" originates from historical warriors who, upon reaching enemy shores, burned their own ships to eliminate any chance of retreat. This mindset forces full commitment, eliminating distractions and fears of failure. When there is no Plan B, your only option is to succeed, and that creates a powerful shift in focus and determination.

Embracing the 'Made by Me' philosophy means understanding that while life throws unexpected challenges, your response to them defines your path. Are you ready to take ownership of your story and rewrite your destiny?

The Hero's Journey – Your Life as a Movie

Imagine your life as a movie. Every great story has a hero, challenges, villains, and a moment of transformation. But the real question is—are you the hero of your story, or just an extra in someone else's?

1. Every Hero Faces a Struggle

In every movie, the hero starts as an ordinary person, unaware of the challenges ahead. Then, something happens—a crisis, a loss, a moment of realization. That's when the journey begins.

Life is the same. You might be stuck in a routine, following what society expects. But real heroes don't just exist—they evolve. They fight battles, learn lessons, and transform themselves.

2. Who Are the Villains in Your Story?

A hero's journey is incomplete without villains. But villains are not always people. Sometimes, they are:

Self-doubt – The voice in your head saying, "You can't do this."

Fear of failure – The fear that keeps you from taking the first step.

Society's expectations – The pressure to follow a "safe" and "normal" life path.

The real battle is not outside—it's inside your mind. The moment you defeat these villains, you take control of your story.

3. The Transformation Moment

In every movie, there's a turning point—a moment where the hero stops running and starts fighting. That's when transformation happens.

Your transformation starts when you take responsibility. When you stop blaming circumstances and start rewriting your story. When you decide that you will not be just a background character but the main protagonist.

4. Your Final Victory

Every hero has a defining moment—the victory that changes everything. But here's the secret: In real life, victory isn't about money, fame, or success. It's about freedom—the freedom to live on your own terms.

So ask yourself:

Are you writing your own script, or is someone else writing it for you?

Are you taking risks, or playing it safe?

Are you becoming the hero of your life story?

Because at the end of the day, life is your movie. And only you can decide how it ends.

Action Plan – How to Write Your Own Story

Step 1: Audit Your Life – Are You Following Someone Else's Script?

Before you start writing your own story, you need to figure out whether you're actually living your own life or just following a script handed to you by society, family, or past experiences.

Ask yourself:

Am I making choices based on what I truly want, or am I trying to meet others' expectations?

If I had no fear of judgment, what would I do differently?

What are the things I tolerate in my life that I don't truly want?

The goal here is to break free from autopilot mode. You can't create a new story if you're stuck in an old one that isn't even yours.

Step 2: "No Plan B" Approach – What's Stopping You?

Most people don't commit fully to their dreams because they keep a safety net—something to fall back on. While this might seem smart, it often weakens commitment and focus. A "No Plan B" mindset forces you to give your 100% because failure is not an option.

To develop this mindset:

Identify what you truly want in life.

Ask yourself: If I had no backup plan, how would I act differently?

Remove distractions and half-hearted commitments that dilute your energy.

Train yourself to handle uncertainty and develop resilience.

The moment you stop seeing failure as a final outcome and start seeing it as part of the journey, you unlock a whole new level of determination.

Step 3: Take Risks, Make Mistakes, but Keep Moving Forward!

No great story is written without challenges. If you're too afraid to make mistakes, you'll never progress.

Take risks – Growth happens outside your comfort zone.

Fail fast, learn faster – Mistakes are proof that you're trying. Don't fear them, embrace them.

Keep moving forward – Even slow progress is better than staying stuck.

Your story will be full of ups and downs, but as long as you're moving forward, you are in control. Start today—write the story you want to live.

The Final Question – What Will Be the Ending of Your Story?

Every great story has an ending. The question is—who is writing yours? Will you take control, shape your destiny, and become the hero of your journey? Or will you remain a supporting character in someone else's script?

Life doesn't hand you a predetermined ending. You create it.

Will you chase your dreams or settle for what's comfortable?

Will you take risks or play it safe forever?

Will you write a story worth remembering or let life write it for you?

At the end of the day, the choice is yours. **"Made by Me" is not just a title; it's an attitude**. It's about owning every chapter of your life—the successes, the failures, the lessons, and the victories.

"So, what will your final chapter look like? Start writing it today."

XIII

DARE, DO, DOMINATE

The 3D Mindset: Dare ▸ Do ▸ Dominate

Why Do Some People Take Risks While Others Stay Stuck?

Success isn't a mystery; it's a mindset. Some people break free from their fears and take bold steps, while others remain trapped in hesitation. The difference? A mindset built on three essential stages: Dare, Do, and Dominate.

The 3 Stages of Success:

1. Dare – Having the courage to start.

2. Do – Taking action consistently.

3. Dominate – Mastering and leading in your field.

If you want to achieve anything extraordinary, you must go through all three stages. Let's break them down.

Dare: Breaking the Fear Barrier

The hardest part of success isn't winning; it's starting. Most people never take the first step because they're paralyzed by fear. But ask yourself: Is the fear of failure worse than the fear of regret?

Fear of failure keeps you stuck. Fear of regret pushes you forward. Which one will you choose?

No one who took action ever regretted trying. But countless people regret never daring to begin.

Bold risk-takers have changed their lives simply by taking that first step. Think of Steve Jobs, Elon Musk, or Oprah Winfrey. None of them had guarantees. They just dared to start.

The First Step is the Hardest—Take It Anyway.

Do: The Discipline of Action

Many people assume success comes from motivation. Wrong. Action beats motivation every time.

Waiting for motivation is a mistake. You won't always feel inspired—take action anyway.

Follow the 70% Rule: Start even when you're not 100% ready. Perfectionism kills progress.

Small daily actions matter more than big one-time efforts. Consistency creates success.

Success isn't about working harder once in a while; it's about showing up every single day. If you stay disciplined in taking action, success becomes inevitable.

Dominate: Becoming the Best

There's a difference between success and domination. Success means reaching a goal; domination means owning the field.

If you want to outperform 99% of people, do what they won't do—stay consistent, keep learning, and push your limits.

The world's best don't just work hard; they work smart and relentlessly.

Repetition is the secret to mastery. The more you do something, the better you get.

Want to be the best? Then make sure you're willing to do what it takes to dominate.

The "No Permission" Mindset

Most people wait for permission. Permission from society, family, or even themselves. But the truth is, you don't need anyone's approval to start.

Stop waiting for validation—just begin.

Society rewards results, not excuses.

Playing it safe is the biggest risk of all. The longer you wait, the harder it becomes.

If you want something, take it. No one is coming to give you permission.

The Final Test: Are You Ready to Dare, Do, Dominate?

Success isn't about luck; it's about action. And now, you have a choice:

What's one bold action you can take today?

What's stopping you from dominating?

Will you dare, or will you wait?

☙

The clock is ticking. Your story is waiting. Dare. Do. Dominate.

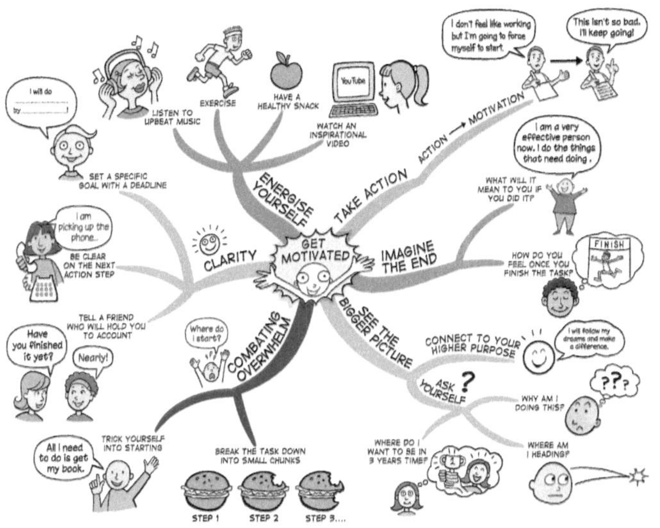

Whenever you feel lost, come back to this map

Take action

Transform your thoughts into actions, fuel your dreams with relentless effort, and watch as you achieve the extraordinary—because success belongs to those who act now, not later

TIME IS NOW

"Time is the most precious resource you have—once it's gone, it's never coming back. So, don't just watch the clock, use every tick to build the life you desire. Every moment is a chance to take action, make progress, and create a future that reflects your true potential."

WRITE YOUR OWN STORY

Don't let anyone else write the chapters of your life. Take control of your narrative, make bold choices, and write your own story—one filled with purpose, passion, and the courage to live it your way.

The end is not the finish line, it's just a new starting point. Every end brings a chance for a fresh beginning, a chance to learn, grow, and move forward. Don't see the end as the end, but as the beginning of something new and exciting. Keep going, because your journey is far from over.

www.ingramcontent.com/pod-product-compliance
Lightning Source LLC
Chambersburg PA
CBHW021527150726
47990CB00006B/2119